DISEASE HOW BRINGS SOCIAL NEGATIVE INFLUENCES

JOHN LOK

First Printing: Jan 2021

Contents

Preface

Introduction

Nowadays, COVID 19 disease had brought human more negative influences, instead of it can bring economic recession to global, it can also bring business losses. The question is that when COVID 19 disease will disappear. If this kind of disease disappeared, when global economy whether it can recover again in order to bring our past economy growth situation.

In my this book, I shall concentrate on discussing cruise, tourism and seeing cinema movie lesisure need aspects, to explain how and why COVID 19 disease may bring serious negative impacts to these three kinds of leisure industry consumer behaviors and lesiure needs. Readers can have more clear understanding how and why COVID 19 disease may influence global leisure future development to be worse to compare economic recession, unemployment rate raising, inflation etc. other factors.

Prologue

Table of content

How COVID 19 disease influences cruise pasengers their tourism leisure on sea to Singapre and Australia cruise leisure passengers number and medical insurace expense is raised ? p.96-107

Can COVI19 disease cause the cruise industry service staffs lose jobs?

How cruise travelers can protect themselves ?

Chapter 5
Illness how influences Economic Recession

COVID 19 disease how influences consumer individual visiting shopping behavior p.108-130

COVID 19 disease how brings online shopping behavior chance

COVID 19 disease how impacts global economic recession on shopping aspect

When economy recovers after COVID disease disappears

CHAPTER ONE

How COVID 19 disease influences tourism leisure need

How and why tourism industry development will be influenced by these possible factors, e.g. pollution, travel stragegy, illness etc. different factors to cause global tourism development will spend how much time to experience growth stage from birth stage, growth stage to mature stage, even decline stage. For example, I shall explain how to prove environmental pollution will influence to the country's tourism industry will experience decline stage from growth stage. I shall attempt to explain how and why COVID 19 disease my be the main factor to influence future tourism industry continue development. It can bring the most serious negavtive impact to influence travellers feel fear to catch air planes to go to any where to travel frequently, even sometimes travelling nowadays, when COVID 19 disease confimed had been caused to attack any countries, e.g. UK, US, China, Korea, etc. countries. But, now, it had been influenced to global tourism industry to bring negative impact to influence travellers to feel fear to catch air planes to go to any where to travel. So, global whole travelling industry is declining, Every country travellers number is decreasing, airline ticket sale number is also decreasing, travel agent income and airline income is also decreasing. Many air planes are needed to stay on every country's airport, but the airlines' air planes, they are needed to pay parking rent to airport. So, expenditure is very much to any airlines.

Why COV19 disease and traveller traveelling lesiure behavior have close relationship ?

Psychological method to predict travel behavioural consumption.

On the psychological view point, I think individual traveler's character will have those kind of personal characteristics. First, simplicity searchers value above everything ease not transparency in their travel planning and holiday making, and are willing to avoid having to go through extensive research. Second, cultural purists use their travel as an opportunity to immerse themselves in an unfamiliar looking to break themselves entirely from their home lives and engage. Sincerely with a different way of living. Third, social capital seekers understand that to be well travelled is a personal quality, and their choices are shaped by their desire to take maximum of social reward from their travel. They will exploit the potential of digital media to enrich and inform their experiences, and structure their adventures always keeping in mind they are being watched by online audiences. Finally, reward hunters seek a return on the investment who make in their busy , high-achieving lives. Linked in part to the growing trend of wellness, including both physical and mental self improvement who seek truly extraordinary and often indulgent or luxurious' must have experiences.

Why needs to know the personal character of individual traveler's characteristics? Because if travel agents could feel which kinds of individual traveler's character, then who can predict which kind of travel package to design to them more easily. For example, how to determine future travel behaviour from past travel experience and perceptions of risk and safety? We need to concern that the influences of past international travel experience, types of risk associated with international travel and the overall degree of safety feeling during international travel on individual's travelling experiences likelihood of travelling to various geographic regions on their next international vacation trip or avoidance of those regions, due to perceived risk. Because individual traveler's experience of safety risk degree to the countries, it will influence who chooses to go to the countries/ country to travel again.

Why COVID 19 disease influences travellers begin to concern green or nature tourism ?

However, green or nature tourism strategy may include these elements : Quality, tourism should have an impact on the quality of life for all members of the tourist process, exploitation of nature resources should be optimal and ensure their generation, balance, distribution of benefits among participants in the tourist process must be fair. So, future any kinds of green or nature tourism will need have these features in order to attract many travelers to visit any countries' green lands, e.g. they may rent cars to travel to green lands. So, developing attractive green lands will be one kind new travelling trend for green tourism in global future travel market.

There are two types of models that contribute to the better understanding of future tourism industry development, explanatory model refer to factors that cause development growth. For example, whether the travelers feel necessary to travel to different destinations, very often nice landscapes and sightseeing, pescriptive modes (e.g. life clcle explanations, physical models) examines tourism from what appears on ground e.g. large hotels facilities etc. Hence, any kinds of tourism leisure must need build these both models in order to attract travelers to choose to buy the tourism package from the travel agent more easily. It is important tourism leisure element to any one travel agent's tourism service package if it hopes to develop its tourism service success. So, the expansion of the tourist region over the natural boundaries of the city centre that occured in the first place as a result of the growth of tourism demand, is the end causing this very expansion to continue.

Butler (1980) involves a six stage evoluation of tourism, namely explanation, involvement, development, consolidation, stagnation, and post-stagnation. The last stage is further characterized by a period of decline, rejuvenation or stabilization. The applicability of the model to a given area has been assessed and judged of a tourist destination's development matched the six phases conceptually described by Butler

reference

Butler, R.W. (1980). the concept of a tourist area cycle of evolution: Implications for management of resources. Canadian Geographer, 24, 5-12.

Hence, our tourism industry is facing decline life cycle stage because COVD 19 human mouth disease has influenced many travelers feel fear to catch airplanes to travel, even they also feel to contact the potential COVD 19 human mouth disease people when they arrive the country , they feel that they may contact these sick people, instead of airplanes. So, this kind disease had influenced many travel agents reduce tourism service package number , due to many travelers' tourism leisure activities will reduce, due to travelers number reduces, they only carry cargos to transport to replace travelers COVD 19 disease influence our tourism industry is experiencing decline life cycle stage nowadays. Unless, COVD 19 human mouth attacking to lung disease can be treated by new medicine invention . Otherwise,

tourism industry can not re-grow to mature life cycle stage easily.
The most used framework for examing stagnation and possible decline in tourism destinations has been tourist area life cycle model (Butler, 1980). The model has been operationalized frequently in the tourism lierature. It includes series of stages in tourism development, leadning eventually to the stagnation and post-stagnation stages. When a nature destination can either decline, however, it does not offer a systematic explanation of hoe tourism destination might avoid decline . Such as COVD 19 human mouth disease may influence travelers feel fear to catch air planes. So, even the country has beautiful nature scene to attract people to travel, althoug it is a nature attractive destination, but due to COVD19 disease occurs, it may influence this country's this nature attractive destination to enter decline life cycle stage at this moment.
Hence, tourism industry's life cycle stage , sometime it can be influenced by non predicted factor, such as COVD19 disease factor, it can influence travelers' travelling desire to be reduced suddenly from 2019 , due to they feel afraid to catch air planes to avoid to get this kind COVD 19 human mouth disease to bring lung disease when they are sitting in closed window inside air plane environment. So, COVD 19 human counth disease causes global tourism industry is facing serious decline life cycle stage. The question is that any one does not know when this kind COVD 19 disease will be treated by new medicine invention, so if this kind COVD 19 disease still can not be killed by new medicine invention, then it will continue to influence global tourism development to be improved , even any nature attractive scenes, they can not persuade any travelers to catch air planes to visit any countries to travel easily. But, however, we still need to keep our natural environment to prepare future COVD 19 diease disappears , e.g. parks are important places for the protection of ecological systems and natural resources as well as for the provision ot recreational and tourism opportunities for the public. Then, nature or green tourism can be continue to develop to attract many travelers to travel after COVD 19 disease disappears in the future.

How COVID 19 disease influences tourism industry recession ?
Butler , R.W. (1980)'s model begins with a discovery and exploration or birth stage in which a location is discovered by a small, select group of people as a place with desirable assets often, this discovery is nature population who may see the perceived assets. As just ordinary aspects of their environment or local culture. The early tourists have very little

support in the form of amenities, and typically, this is preferred and is part of a location's of being undiscovered. The early tourists, therefore rely heavily on and interact frequently with the residents of the region. This small group of early tourists is largely in dependent and shares information about a destination by word of mouth or by select affinity groups. Over time, as more people are introduced to the destination, the number of visitors begins to increase. So " word of mouth" will be traveler information to persuade them to make travelling destination choices in the tourism industry beginning. It is tourism industry's birth life cycle stage characteristics . However, internet invention can let any one see any countries' scene photos, so it is one kind of good advertisement method to introduce any countries' scene, instead of travelling magazine in tourism growth and maturity life cucle both stages.

Why senior age will be main travelling target after COV19 disease attacks to global tourism lesiure need?

In the past, Germany government had established tourism survey analysis to analyze survey data in order to arrive at reliable conclusions on future trends in travel behavior. To aim to find how demographic change will influence the tourism market and how the industry can adapt to those changes. The travel analysis provided data on tourism consumer behavior, including attitudes, motives and intentions. Since, 1970 year, it is based on a random sample, representative for the population in private households aged 14 years or older. Then, a continuous high scientific standard combined with a national and international users makes the travel analysis a useful tool and reliable source for tourism industry and policy decisions. It aimed to gather statistical data. e.g. on the age structure and on demographic trends, quantitative and qualitative analysis with time series data from the travel analysis. It shows e.g. not only the future volume , quite different from today's seniors, or how who will travel of family holidays will change, e.g. single parents of low, but grandparents of growing significance for tourism.

Demographic change is said to be one of the important drivers for new trends in consumer traveling change behavior in most European countries (e.g. Lind 2001). Because the growing number of senior citizens in the European Union and other industralised countries, such as the USA and Japan, looks to become one of the major marketing challenges for the tourism industry. United Nations statistics predict that the share of people being 60 age or older will grow dramatically in the coming future, and is expected to rise from 10 percent of the world population in 2000 year to more than 20 percent in 2050 year (United Nations Population Division, 2001). From its statistic, some data showed that travel propensity increased throughout life until the age of about 50 years of age and was then kept stable until very late in life 75 age. The most important results is that the travel propensity when getting older is not going down between 65 and 75 age of course, the overall development of this variable is influenced by a lot of other factors which are rsponsible for quite a variation over time. It is now possible to suggest that the general pattern of travel propensity is one of the key indicators for holiday life cycle travel behaviour, includes three stages. The growth stage tends to increase from early aduithood until 45 age old or when reaching some 80%. The next stage is stabilisation from the ages of around 50 age,until 75 age old, starting with a lower increase. Finally, the decrease stage is a slight decrease occurs once people reach the more advanced age of 75 age to 85 age old (Lohmann & Danielsson 2001).

So, it seems Germany government tourism prediction to future travellers' behaviour indicated these findings, such as on how future senior generations will travel, who had used survey data to examine the patterns of travel behaviour of a generation getting older and applied the findings to draw conclusions on the future. Also, it predicted that on the future of family trips, family semgmentation will be the travel behaviour patterns in the future. These findings together with the statistical data on demographic change allowed for a better understanding of the coming tends in family holidays. It's aim developed in consumer behaviour related to demographic change and predicted what will happen future of tourism one had to consider other influences and drivers as well, for example, trends on the supply side. e.g. low cost airlines or in travelling consumption behaviour in general whether how the past may provide a key to predict travel patterns of senior sitizens to the future.

Given the projected growth of the senior citizens market, designing specific marketing strategies to meet the prospective needs of elderly tourists will become increasingly important. It has been an implict assumption that it will be a close relationship between the travel behaviour of today's senior citizens and the those of future ones. The growing number of senior citizens in the world. e.g. China, Hong Kong, Japan, USA etc. countries. Global senior citizen tourism market will be based solely on demographic predictions about the future of the population's age structure. However, many of these seniors won't only live longer but will be fitter and more active until later in life. Many of the will also have plenty in life. Many of them will also have plenty of time and money to spend on travel. So, will these new seniors behave like today's senior citizens? Will they adopt the same travel behaviour as the previous generation or become a new market of oldies for the leisure and tourism indudtry? However, to determine the actual number of senior citizens who will be travelling and to sought to evaluate and specify certain difficult to predict the actual numbers of senior citizen to any country. However, they can be based on the implicit assumption that there is a close relationship between the travel behaviour of past, present and future seniors. But is this a valid assumption? As the reiseanalyse travel analysis survey, which was conducted in Germany every year, offered some interesting data possibiltieis. It was designed to monitor the holiday travel behaviour, opinions and attitudes of Germans and has been carried out since 1970 year, questions in the questionnaire. Data are based on face to face interviews, with a representative sample of more than 7,500 repondents, the interviews being carried out in January each year. All results refer to the average for the defined generated, which ranges generally over ten years. The group of people then at the age of 60 to 69 age is described. This corresponds to the same generation ten years ago, when they had an age of 50 to 59 age. When this methodological approach is not necessarily very sophisticated, it does have the important advantages of being cost effective. Thus, COVD19 disease can influence future senior age traveller personal tourism leisure need raise, because they may feel COVID 19 disease can not be caused to disappear in short time. They are fear death, so they will choose to go to any where to travel before they die. So, future global tourism industry's main customer target may be old age people more than young age people.

Hence, our tourism industry is facing decline life cycle stage because COVD 19 human mouth disease has influenced many travelers feel fear to catch airplanes to travel, even they also feel to contact the potential COVD 19 human mouth disease people when they arrive the country , they feel that they may contact these sick people, instead of airplanes. So, this kind disease had influenced many travel agents reduce tourism service package number , due to many travelers' tourism leisure activities will reduce, due to travelers number reduces, they only carry cargos to transport to replace travelers COVD 19 disease influence our tourism industry is experiencing decline life cycle stage nowadays. Unless, COVD 19 human mouth attacking to lung disease can be treated by new medicine invention . Otherwise, tourism industry can not re-grow to mature life cycle stage easily.

The most used framework for examing stagnation and possible decline in tourism destinations has been tourist area life cycle model (Butler, 1980). The model has been operationalized frequently in the tourism lierature. It includes series of stages in tourism development, leadning eventually to the stagnation and post-stagnation stages. When a nature destination can either decline, however, it does not offer a systematic explanation of hoe tourism destination might avoid decline . Such as COVD 19 human mouth disease may influence travelers feel fear to catch air planes. So, even the country has beautiful nature scene to attract people to travel, althoug it is a nature attractive destination, but due to COVD19 disease occurs, it may influence this country's this nature attractive destination to enter decline life cycle stage at this moment.

Hence, tourism industry's life cycle stage , sometime it can be influenced by non predicted factor, such as COVD19 disease factor, it can influence travelers' travelling desire to be reduced suddenly from 2019 , due to they feel afraid to catch air planes to avoid to get this kind COVD 19 human mouth disease to bring lung disease when they are sitting in closed window inside air plane environment. So, COVD 19 human counth disease causes global tourism industry is facing serious decline life cycle stage. The question is that any one does not know when this kind COVD 19 disease will be treated by new medicine invention, so if this kind COVD 19 disease still can not be killed by new medicine invention, then it will continue to influence global tourism development to be improved , even any nature attractive scenes, they can not persuade any travelers to catch air planes to visit any countries to travel easily. But, however, we still need to keep our natural environment to prepare future COVD 19 diease disappears , e.g. parks are important places for the protection of ecological systems and natural resources as well as for the provision ot recreational and tourism opportunities for the public. Then, nature or green tourism can be continue to develop to attract many travelers to travel after COVD 19 disease disappears in the future.

● What are the characteristics of future tourism industry changes after COVID 19 disease disappears?

Butler , R.W. (1980)'s model begins with a discovery and exploration or birth stage in which a location is discovered by a small, select group of people as a place with desirable assets often, this discovery is nature population who may see the perceived assets. As just ordinary aspects of their environment or local culture. The early tourists have very little support in the form of amenities, and typically, this is preferred and is part of a location's of being undiscovered. The early tourists, therefore rely heavily on and interact frequently with the residents of the region. This small group of early tourists is largely in dependent and shares information about a destination by word of mouth or by select affinity groups. Over time, as more people are introduced to the destination, the number of visitors begins to increase. So " word of mouth" will be traveler information to persuade them to make travelling destination choices in the tourism industry beginning. It is tourism industry's birth life cycle stage characteristics . However, internet invention can let any one see any countries' scene photos, so it is one kind of good advertisement method to introduce any countries' scene, instead of travelling magazine in tourism growth and maturity life cucle both stages.

Moreover, space tourism is at the birth life cycle stage. It needs travelers feel interest to travel space, if this kind space tourism service providers hope to implement their any space journeys in success. These factors may influence its development succeeds. Nowadays, its target market is wealthy travelers group, wealthy individual are needed, as they serve as the main consumers for space tourism . For space tourism to succeed there must be enough demand from those who are able to afford to expensive ticket. To date there have only been seven commercial space travelers, or space tourists, although they prefer to be called space flight participant, as they see themselves as pioneers and adventers as opposed to ordinary tourists. So, any future space tourism that price must need to reduce to general public, e.g. ordinary income level people, they can spend, if space tourism hopes to reach from stage stage rapidly. So, space tourism is still far to mature stage.It depends on whether how long time its any space journey ticket price can be reduced to any one can pay. So, when its customer target is not only wealthy travelers, many ordinary or common income level people, they can pay to any one space jounrney. It may mean to reach growth life cycle stage.

CHAPTER TWO

How COVID 19 disease bring space tourism industry development

- The space tourism leisure need may raise after COVID 19 disease disappears

When human space tourism of commericalization of activities in outer space can bring these feeling to let any one space traveler feels then, it may mean that it can reach growth stage, such as they may feel their any space journeys may bring positive impacts that outer. Space recreation can produce, in order to come up with space tourism, exploring and untravelling the hidden anystories of the space are needed. Also they can feel need drastically broadens and enrichs human's technical awareness and constructive knowledge need from any one space tourism journey package. When space tourism reachs mature life cycle stage? What its characteristics are? When any one space travelers can feel that not only earth based attractions that simulate the space experience , they must need to catch airships to experience this different tourism experience, such as space theme parks, space training camps, virtual reality facilities , space hotels (skotel), multimedia interactive games and tele robotic moon rovers controlled from earth, but also parabolic flights, lasting up to three days or week long stay at floating space hotel, including participatory educational ,as well as sports competitions (i.e. space olympics). Hence, above these will be nay space tourism development. It can reach mature life cycle stage characteristics when any one can feel the real travelling mouth to compare to travel our earth anywhere, they can not find that they feel space tourism may be same to our earth's holiday (need to rela) or cultural (know different places or specialized tourism, e.g. expectations of adventures , even space scientists discover new experiences to expectations of adventure or get more information, scientific interest feeling. Then, at this moment, we can call space tourism has reached the mature stage. However, I believe that to develop space tourism in success. We must need to control space tourism ticket price to be reduced to general low income people. They may spend budget level. So, ticket price may be one major factor to influence future space tourism growth when it can reach mature stage. Also, it mean that whether space tourism may become another kind of popular tourism lesiure activities to use. It depends on ticket price factor, instead of its any space tourism trip arrangement factor. So, any one space tourism service provider must need long time to spend in order to implement its different strategies, e.g. ticket price, space trip arrangemet to achieve its their space tourism to achieve its their space tourism different destination package in success if they hope their future space tourism business can grow up in short time.

Why does COVD19 disease influences future space tourism leisure need raises?

- Psychology and economic environment changing both factors influence whole space tourism market leisure desire

How can psychology method predict space tourism leisure desire? I believe that it has relationship between the space tourism planner and the economic environment as well as his/her psychology as below:
Firstly, on the economic environment influence hand, it includs these both economic situations, either in the good economic environment, many people can earn high income and employers can supply many job number to provide to many people to work, then it will influence the space travelling planner has more space travelling desire. Otherwise, or in the bad economic, less people can earn high income and employers can not supply many job number to provide to many people to work, it will influence the space travelling planner has less space travelling desire.
Secondly, on these both the space travelling planner individual psychology influence hand, the space travelling planner will have these both aspects of individual psychological influence, it includes these both either positive or negative psychological influence aspectsas below:
On the positive psychological influence aspect, if the space travelling

planner has confidence to the space travelling leisure company can provide safe, comfortable, good quality of one space travelling trip arrangement, good taste food arrangement, reasonable space ticket price and every reasonable space trip for space hotel living arrangement and space garden and space farming land visiting journey arrangement, even, space swimming pool and space sport centre and space cinema leisure arrangement to let whom to stay on the planet at least one day trip, it means not one short time space trip, e.g. the spacecraft only flies about half hour or one half. It can not fly to the planet to arrive its space station destination to stay to let the space travelling planner to live at the space hotel at least one night. Then the space travelling planner will have more desire to choose to catch the space tourism leisure company's spacecraft to travel to space.
Otherwise, on the negative psychological influence aspect, if the space travelling planner lacks confidence to the space travelling leisure company can provide safe, comfortable, good quality of one space travelling trip arrangement, good taste food arrangement, reasonable space ticket price and every reasonable space trip for space hotel living arrangement and space garden and space farming land visiting journey arrangement, even, space swimming pool and space sport centre and space cinema leisure arrangement to let whom to stay on the planet at least one day trip, it means not one short time space trip, e.g. the spacecraft only flies about half hour or one half. It can not fly to the planet to arrive its space station destination to stay to let the space travelling planner to live at the space hotel at least one night. Then the space travelling planner will have less desire to choose to catch the space tourism leisure company's spacecraft to travel to space.
Hence, it seems economic environment changing factor and the space travelling planner's confidence factor to the space tourism leisure providers will influence the whole space travelling market whose space travelling consumer's space travelling leisure consumption desire to be more or less. So, any one space tourism provider can not neglect these both factors how to influence whose customer consumption desire.

● space tourism strategy

Future any space tourism leisure business needs have good business plan to outline the space tourism leisure business in these aspects , such as: different space tourism destinations of every space tourism journey, technical , financial and regulatory factors for growing space tourism leisure consumption into any one kind of unique artificial intelligent space tourism journey for identified passenger target group.

All how to design one space tourism business development plan to attempt to predict whether what trends will influence how every different kinds of identified space tourism journey in order to achieve passenger number growing aim as well as how to achieve one attractive space tourism leisure to satisfy future space tourism passenger individual space travel needs more easily.

I shall indicate what aspects to future every space tourism traveler who will consider in order to reduce the space tourism traveler personal worry to catch any pace boats to leave our Earth to fly to other planets to travel.

I recommend that any space tourism leisure organizations need to concern these aspects in their space tourism leisure business plan as below:

(1) safe space tourism journey

On first aspect concerns safe space tourism journey plan to let all space tourism travelers will considerate safe issue. They must ensure space boats that is safe to catch them to fly to planets in their space journeys. So, any space tourism leisure business will utilize previous flight rated and proven technologies to form the basis for manufacturing spacecraft vehicles, and will incorporate the latest modern avionics and flight systems for ensuring safety, reliability and economical operation in order to reduce any space tourism traveler personal worry to catch any spacecraft.

So, the space tourism safe journey plan is one very important factor to influence space tourism consumer number for them if any one of space tourism leisure business hoped they can grow the space tourism consumer number for long term. For example, the space boat flight hardware must often be maintained at the space station. It is needed to be considered by space boat experts as risky, extremely expensive and potentially sensitive. To aims to ensure spacecraft will offer an economical and safe alternative for any satellite manufacturers and other space tourism entertainment organizations have a desire or requirement for space tourism flight.

(2) reduction cost expense plan

On second aspect concerns reduction cost expense plan, any space tourism entertainment organizations need have the experience and capacity for safely launching a fully loaded , including space tourism passengers and passenger individual cargo for every spacecraft tourism journey. As a result of outsourcing the launch role to a major contractor, the space tourism pilot can concentrate on space boat crews flight training, planning space tourism passenger cargo capacity and preparing space flight manifests , and will as a result, avoid the expense of maintaining a launch operation on a daily basis. In addition, by outsourcing the spacecraft manufacturing, it can avoid spending millions of dollar on facilities and equipment infrastructure and engineering manufacturing expertise.

(3) achieve any space tourism mission plan
On third aspect concerns how to achieve any space tourism mission. Every space tourism mission must be ensure that reliable service is provided to satisfy every space tourism passenger personal space traveler needs and let them to enjoy in their whole space tourism journey, let them to catch a big aircraft in comfortable environment of technologically sophisticated space boat, reasonable and competitive every time space tourism flight ticket price plan is developed and properly revised every time space tourism ticket price when performing their assigned every different space tourism journey mission.
Hence, the space tourism leisure company will provide one careful selected space tourism destination , e.g. Mar planet space tourism journey, Moon planet space tourism journey or no any space destination journey, it means that the space craft only needs to fly one circle around between Earth and Moon space journey etc. that are capable of meeting the requirements of travelling into Earth orbit. So, any space tourism journey must emphasize affordability, reliability, safety, customer service and responsiveness in responding to every client's space tourism journey requirements. Hence, any one of space tourism journey must have clear space journey mission and objective to satisfy any space traveler client target needs.

1.1 Methods to raise space traveler number

Future space tourism will be one kind of new travel leisure market for any new space travel leisure companies to enter this undiscovered market in the beginning. However, how to predict future 10 to 20 years , even more space traveler number that is one important issue to any new space tourism leisure companies.
I think that space tourism leisure companies need to define what kinds of space travel leisure service to be provided to space travelling passengers, however, what age group of space passengers who will be their space travelling target client. For example, their space travel leisure must provide any flight operation that takes one or more passengers beyond the altitude of 100 km and thus into space to let space travelling passengers who have

fun, exciting space travelling feeling.
Anyway, for any kind of space tourism (leisure space travel) journey, space tourism leisure company needs anyone to be bring customer satisfaction, it is a plan or predictive methods to measure how to let every space travelling passenger to feel comfortable when they are catching the spacecraft (space flying product) and they can have enjoyable and fun or exciting feeling when they have need providing any space tourism journey, services meet or surpass customer expectations.
Thus, any space tourism leisure company needs to evaluate the degree of every time space tourism journey's customer satisfaction and customer satisfaction is also always evaluated in relationship to the every time ticket price of the space tourism journey. So, the space tourism leisure company will predict the next time of what the space tourism journey of passenger number is more accurate, after it has evaluated what degree of every time space tourism journey's customer satisfaction is. It aims to gather their opinions to find which aspects that they need to revise, e.g. choosing where will be the next time space tourism journey destination, how to improve spacecraft staff's service attitude and performance to serve to their space tourism passengers when they are catching the spacecraft, to evaluate whether the spacecraft can provide comfortable and safe environment to let them to catch in order to let the next time space travelling passengers can feel satisfactory and enjoyable when they are catching the space tourism leisure's spacecraft to fly to anywhere in space.

In general, the expectation of factors space passengers include the following customer value elements, such as below:

- viewing space and the Earth.
- experiencing weightlessness and being able to float freely in zero gravity.
- experiencing pre-flight astronaut training and related sensations.
- communicating from space to significant others.
- being able to discuss the adventure in an informed way.
- having astronaut like documentation and memorabilia.

These objectives need to be combined with, sometimes conflicting constraints, such as guaranteed safe return, limited training time, reasonable comfort, and minimum medical restrictions. All these above issues which will be every space travelling passenger considerate matters before they choose the space tourism leisure company to catch its spacecraft to fly to space. So, all these factors will influence the next time space passenger number. Any space tourism leisure company can not neglect how to solve these all matters before they decide when their next time space tourism journey to be achieved.

Consequently, if the space craft tourism leisure company could revise what aspects of its last space tourism journey to find what are its wrong or weakness or unattractive challenges to cause any one space travelling passenger who feels unsatisfactory. Then, it can have more effort to concentrate on improving its next space tourism journey to raise its space tourism service performance level , e.g. people, food, leisure etc. service aspects and its space tourism product quality level, e.g. proving comfortable spacecraft facilities to let space travelling passengers to catch in whole spacecraft tourism journey. Then, it will have more confidence to achieve the raising space travelling passenger number.

● What is the prediction space travelling passenger desire method ?

The prediction space travelling passenger individual desire method can be one survey investigation method. When every time spacecraft finishes space tourism journey mission, after all space tourism passengers catch the spacecraft to arrive earth from space. When they arrive earth space station destination, then the space tourism leisure company can arrange survey investigation staffs to enquire their feeling for this time space tourism journey immediately.

The survey content can include as below:

Do you feel satisfactory or unsatisfactory to which aspects of this time space tourism journey?

(1) On service aspect questions include as below:

(a) Do you feel space food taste is good?

(b) Do you enjoy this time space tourism journey arrangement?

(c) Do you feel satisfactory to space staff
service performance?

(d) If you have unsatisfactory feeling for any one of above questions, which aspect issue cause you feel unsatisfactory to explain to let us to know in order to us to revise our service performance.

(2) On product aspect questions include as below:

(a) Do you feel comfortable when you are catching our spacecraft in whole space tourism journey?

(b) If you feel comfortable , may you explain the reasons what aspects of our spacecraft has weakness to cause you feel uncomfortable?

(c) Do you feel safe when you are catching our spacecraft in whole space tourism journey?

(d) If you feel unsafe, may you explain the reasons what aspects of our spacecraft has weakness to cause you feel unsafe?

Finally, we thank your ideas to be given to let us know how to improve our every time future space tourism journey in order to find what challenge cause our service performance and product quality which can not satisfy your needs. So, we shall improve to avoid future challenges continue occur. Our mission is achievement of 100% satisfactory level to our every space travelling passenger individual feeling. Also, we hope that you can choose our space tourism leisure service again, when you have another time space tourism leisure desire need. However, we shall revise to improve our service performance and product quality to be better, after collecting your ideas from this time survey investigation. I think you spend time to give your ideas from this survey investigation faithfully.

So, survey investigation method will be one important idea gathering tool to help any space tourism leisure company to revise the weaknesses to raise or improve future every time space tourism journey service performance and product quality to achieve raising competitive effort in this new space tourism leisure market.

Hence, survey investigation method will be the best idea gathering method to predict how space travelling passenger emotion or desire need will change in order to achieve the objective of raising every time space tourism journey future space travelling passenger number more easily for every space tourism leisure company.

● How does price factor won't be the main factor to influence space traveler number when COVID 19 disease brings negative emotion to travellers ?

The space tourism leisure organizations indicate the total cost of a trip into space is rapidly coming down from the initial price level of about US$600,000, it is obvious that the space travelling customer base is going to be rather small. Typical customers tend to belong to the top 1% income bracket. They also indicate that the price comes down , it is expected that new space travelling customer groups will enter the space tourism leisure market.

Typical new customers include people in other brackets with one-of-a kind incomes, such as inheritance or business sold. There are indications that those types of customers are becoming interested in spending on an once-in-a lifetime space experience. Therefore, the growth of the space tourism market is highly sensitive to customer satisfaction and how it is communicated through various media.

This will establish the status factors of space tourism and corresponding brand reputation service providers. They also suggest that any operator monitors space travelling customer satisfaction closely, as it will help developing increasingly accurate estimates of how the space tourism leisure market will develop.

Hence, it seems that every time space tourism journey price variable factor will influence the time space tourism of customer individual leisure desire and the space tourism passenger number. For example, the minimum price goal foe a variable space tourism business is currently estimate to be below US$3000-4000/kg for a round -trip depending on variable configuration and operation size. At this price, they estimate that somewhat over 1 % of the high income earners are potential customers.

However, for significant volume growth the longer term goal should be below US$2000/kg for a typical passenger, baggage and supplies. The lower price will probably open space tourism to a broader population, expanding the customer base and altering expectations. beyond this point space tourism will become into a travelling competitive leisure commodity, price competition will ensure and service providers need to rethink their space tourism marketing and branding and price strategies.

I shall also recommend how to attract the potential customers successfully. First, space operators need to pay special attention to the right level of customer services. Second, various preparatory customer operations cost, such as a travel to the launch site, space tourism destination accommodation, pre-flight training, medical check-ups and equipment my add up to between 10 to 15 % of the actual space travel cost. Thurs, solving the right balance between services offered and cost of client operation in order to earn the largest intangible benefits, such as loyalty, confidence, leisure enjoyment, comfortable space travelling journey as well as tangible benefits, such as profit, spacecraft manufacturing facilities, space stations, space hotels , space swimming pools, space gardens, space cinema etc. which are built to similar to earth building facilities to satisfy space travelers‘ needs.

1.2 The influential factors persuade travelers choose space tourism

Nowadays, our earth is no longer an adventurous enough place for some experienced tourists. Space tourism will be a new sector of adventure tourism, which is in the near future will be fast becoming a new tourism leisure opportunity for experiencing the unknown. Of one day, space tourism is able to reach the mass tourism phase, due to improved safety and decreased operation costs, a future space tourist will possibly only need minimal training to cope with the zero cost.

Space tourism is quite well established with visits to space attraction and launch sites, and it is a wealthy trips to the international space station for any space tourism travelers. However, if any space tourism leisure companies can attempt to find what the most influential factors are to persuade travelers feel attraction more than travelling in our earth.

It aims to let travelers to choose space travelling more than earth travelling when they feel travelling leisure need. I shall indicate what will be the most important influential factors to persuade travelers to choose space tourism more than earth tourism as below:

Firstly, I shall argue that the majority of different new space tourism journey destinations will be needed to find to satisfy different aged space travelers and different income space tourism consumers' needs. For example, the rich people have effort to consume longer time and reach any space tourism destinations where are far away from our earth of their every space tourism journey.

Otherwise, the middle income people will choose shorter space tourism journey distance from our earth and short time space tourism journey. Also, younger space tourism clients can accept more longer journey time, exciting fast speed spacecraft flying journey. Otherwise, old space tourism clients can only accept comfortable and shorter time safe space journey. So, it seems that safety, comfortable feeling, shorter time space tourism journey won't be one important influential factor to excite any young people who choose to consume space tourism leisure. Otherwise, safety, comfortable feeling, shorter time space tourism journey will be one important influential factor to excite any old people who choose to consume space tourism leisure.

Secondly, the another most important influential factor to excite space travelers to choose space tourism , it concerns whether the space travelers will feel what tourists benefits can be earned from a substantial variety of destinations choice. In general, space tourism with those of aviation, space travelers will hope space tourism will be travelling distances by air in a very short time, safely and comfortably, to bring them to arrive any space planet destinations when spacecraft reaches any space stations to stay in any space destinations.

Hence, space destination factor will bring important influential choice to any space destination journeys. As a result of the space technological tourism boom, the number of potential different space destination, choice attractions have grown with far fewer places on earth to which human do have access yet. However, the ultimate different space destinations to which many of us dream is not on earth, but as least 100 km above us, anywhere in space any planets.

If the space tourism leisure company can provide different space tourism destination choices to young or old age both space traveler target consumer groups. They will feel a real holiday when they will be able to enjoy a great image of the earth from planets. It might mean that every space tourism journey can provide different space tourism destination to let space travelers have another new travelling destinations where are far from our earth anywhere.

Hence, the different space tourism destinations will give them an unforgettable adventure. Think of how it would be to be able to check in at a " billion strategy" luxury hotel in space one planet, it means that the space planet destination can provide one luxury hotel to let space travelers to live one night or more in the space planet destination, how it would be to schedule the space traveler' vacation at one of the space tourism leisure company luxury resorts on the Moon or Mars.

This images seem from science fiction movies, but one should not forget that 100 years ago, the Wright brothers, aviation pioneers inventors and builders of the air plane, would not have imagined how, every day it is possible that future spacecraft can fly to any planets to let human have chance to stay in the space hotel one night or more.

Consequently, space destination choice and space tourism journey service performance, aviation safety, ticket price and leisure satisfactory feeling which will be important influential factors to attract future space travelers to choose space tourism leisure to replace earth tourism leisure in future one day.

1.3 Raising space tourism leisure consumption strategies

Although, space tourism industry is a real enjoyment and exciting travelling leisure to human. It is possible that human will choose to consume space tourism leisure to replace earth tourism leisure, if human felt that earth tourism leisure is not attractive to them to consume to go to anywhere to travel in their leisure time.

But, I believe that space tourism industry has still many factors to influence human to choose to consume space tourism leisure, even they will consider space tourism leisure consumption I is only one time space tourism in their life time. Hence, space tourism companies ought achieve this aim to persuade or attract everyone prefer to spend space tourism leisure at least one time in their life, then it can represent success. However, I think to achieve this aim, it has these challenges to influence their success, even they believe space tourism leisure business is one potential attractive travel entertainment business. These challenges include such as: expensive space tourism ticket price issue, catching spacecraft safe issue, space traveler personal body health issue, age issue, family and friend relationship influence issue, working time and holiday time arrangement issue, the space trip arrangement issue, weather issue etc. different challenges, which will have possible to influence every space tourism planner either who decide change to cancel the time space tourism plan, or forgive to choose space tourism leisure in their life forever.

Hence, how to raise space tourism leisure consumption desire will be one considerable matter for any space tourism leisure businessmen. I shall indicate my personal three aspect of strategical opinions to let them to know how to raise every space tourism planner individual space tourism leisure consumption desire to avoid every time space tourism passenger number will have decrease failure chance as below:

● (1) Strategic opinion

On the first aspect of strategic opinion, I feel that the space education tutor can teach new space knowledge to let every space traveler to learn any new space and earth knowledge during he/she is catching on the spacecraft in personal contact learning experience environment which can raise space tourism consumption desire. The reason is because the space tourism leisure traveler can raise extra space and earth learning knowledge when they can catch the spacecraft to fly and contact the space environment to learn and feel what the differences are between space and earth by himself or herself. Hence, it is very attractive to the space traveler student target group and I believe that their parents will encourage their sons or daughters to participate the time of space trip and they are more preferable to help them to buy the time space trip ticket, due to their sons and daughters can learn any space knowledge when they are studying. Moreover, every space traveler will feel surprise to learn any new space and earth knowledge from the space tutor's teaching, due to he/she is unknown that this space travel trip includes learning space and earth knowledge.

I suggest that the space tourism leisure businessmen can give learning opportunity to every travel trip space travelers to feel that this space actual environment can bring what disadvantages or advantages to influence our earth when they are catching aircraft to fly to space to travel in every space trip. The space and earth learning knowledge can include these two aspects of space learning knowledge and experience below:

On the teaching of space environment learning knowledge hand, the topics can include as below:

Firstly the space learning topic can concern how space environment influences water and hydrated minerals change , they can learn what our drinking water function how is applied to space environment. For example, in the space environment, they can learn and attempt to feel that how water can be used in protecting astronauts against harmful radiation from the sun and cosmic rays by cloaking spacecraft with a thin layer of water in the actual space environment as well as the space travelers can also feel water is same as fuel when they are catching the spacecraft, they can feel the water is heavy to transport into space when they are catching the spacecraft to fly to space during their whole space tourism journey.

Moreover, when their spacecraft reaches anyone of planets and it stays on the planet's space station, e.g. Moon space station. They can learn how to attempt to contact the hydrated minerals to learn and feel what they contained in some asteroids may be possible sources of water and fuel in the actual space environment. When they are walking in actual space environment, such as Moon planet, they can contact or touch this hydrated minerals to learn how water molecules can be extracted and separated chemically to produce hydrogen fuel knowledge in the actual space environment. This is one exciting space learning experience to the space travelling student passengers.

Secondly the space learning topic can concern how human fights space threats , even when their whole space leisure journey, the space science teacher can let the space trip student passengers to feel that they are learning new space knowledge between the space science teacher and whose space trip student passengers. Such as how to protect our earth knowledge: Teaching them to know when will be threats to our earth from space. The space science teacher can explain how this space threating environment influences our life safety and let them to feel that a mass extinction can be triggered if an asteroid 10 kilometers across hit the earth. Even being the apex species in the food chain did not space carnivorous dinosaurs from such disaster, who knows if this terrifying scene won't happen before our eyes? So, the space travelers can image and feel how the space threating environment can influence their life safety in the actual space environment as well as the space science teacher can let whose space travelers to feel and image the actual earth disaster will possible happen suddenly to let they feel afraid in the actual space environment. Also the space science teacher can teach how our earth can fright the space stones attack to let the space traveler to know, when an impactor targets an asteroid for a controlled well-times wallop. The collision will change the asteroid's momentum, deflecting it from its original orbital path which intersects with that of the earth. So, at the moment, the space travelers can image they are a larger spacecraft near an asteroid which can also change the path. Given enough time, the gravitational pull from the spacecraft will be able to steer the asteroid away from the earth. So, every space traveler will feel that they are catching the spacecraft in the safe space environment to avoid the Earth disaster from space sudden unpredictable attack.

It is more fun real space tourism knowledge learning feel to let every space traveler has chance to learn any new space science knowledge when he/she is catching the spacecraft to fly to space to travel. Hence, one successful space trip ought include trip and learning experience both contents in order to raise every the space tourism planner individual space trip consumption desire.

- (2) Strategic opinion

On the second aspect of strategic opinion, space tourism leisure companies need to let planning travelers feel that anyone of space tourism leisure is very different to general tourism leisure. In general, tourism leisure is visiting at least one night for leisure and holiday, business or other tourism purposes in Earth only. Otherwise, space tourism leisure is other kind of an unique trip leisure or entertainment method, e.g. the space traveler can catch the spacecraft to visit any planets to stay to live at the planet's space hotel at least one night, e.g. Future potential populated Moon or Mars space hotel space trip. Moreover, the space travel companies ought give chance to let them to feel what weightless feeling is in weightlessness environment when they are walking on Moon or other planets in possible. Even, they can attempt to build these entertainment facilities, instead of space hotels, such as space swimming pools, space gardens, space cinema etc. building facilities. It aims to let them to feel what the differences between Earth and space life when they are walking on the Moon, when they are swimming on the space pools, when they are living in space hotels, when they are watching movies in space cinemas, when they are seeing flowers and different species of planets and fruits. e.g. oranges, apples, bananas, and vegetable and potatoes and tomatoes in space gardens. It is very exciting and fun space trip life experience between one days to seven days. So, they believe that they must not feel these space life experience if they do not choose to participate this time space trip planning journey by the space trip company preparation.

Also, due to that the space tourism passengers need to the pre-flight checks and training before they ensure to qualify to permit to participate the space trip. So space travel companies need to concern how to take care their health check and training matter considerately. It aims to let every space traveler will feel a market segment with fitness and extreme experiences as well as he/she will become popular with a market segment passenger to the space tourism leisure company, although he/she must not guarantee to pass the space training and/or pre-flight health checks to permit to participate the space trip. However, he/she can believe that he/she is one worth space travelling passenger to the space tourism leisure company, even this time pre-flight health check or/and the short time space trip training requirements are failure. However, the space tourism leisure company must need to let all pre-flight health check and space trip training passengers to feel that it is only one space tourism which can give them and let customers view the space travel is as the ultimate showcase for health, even though a majority of the population can pass the pre-flight medical and other tests in order to raise their confidence and safety to catch the spacecraft to fly to space to travel when they are confirmed to pass these tests to permit to catch the spacecraft later.

In general, the expectations of future space passengers include the following customer value elements, such as below:

- Viewing space and the Earth.
- Experiencing weightlessness and experiencing pre-flight astronaut training and related sensations.
- Communicating from space to significant others.
- Being able to discuss the adventure in an informed way.
- Having astronaut-like documentation and memorabilia.
- Enjoying one exciting and fun space trip.

However, instead of considering these objectives need to be combined with, sometimes conflicting , constraints such as guaranteed safe, return , limited training time, reasonable comfort, and minimum medical restrictions. So, space tourism companies need to reduce every space traveler individual worries before they decide to make the time of space tourism journey. Then, it can increase their confidence to raise their space tourism consumption desire more successfully.

Consequently, instead of these consideration, a space travel operator must pay attention to the total customer experience over the entire customer process, starting from how the service is presented, proposed and sold. The service package must include training, instructions, travel to the launch site and various post. Travel activities to generate maximum customer satisfaction and brand building opportunity.

● (3) Strategic opinion

On the final aspect of strategic opinion, I think any space tourism companies space tourism companies need to consider every time space tourism ticket price and space tourism trip issues. It is important factor to influence every space traveler individual consumption desire. Due to space trip ticket price must be more expensive to compare common Earth trip travelling ticket price, so this kind of tourism leisure market target customer will be the rich and high income customer group.

On the space trip ticket challenge issue, despite that fact the total cost of a trip into space is rapidly coming down from the initial price level of about US$60,000, it is obvious that the customer base is going to be rather small and the client target customer is only high income or rich consumer group. Typical customers tend to belong to the top of the top 1% income bracket. So, ensures that space traveler number must be less than common Earth traveler number.

Also, such as the space trip ticket price, it is expected that new middle rich level or middle high level income customer target group will enter the space trip leisure market, when every space trip ticket price falls down about 1% Typical new customers include people in other income brackets with one-of-a-kind incomes, such as inheritance or business sold space traveler target group. These people will be space travel new client group, when its every space trip ticket price can be reduced to close 1 to 2 % nearly. If any space tourism leisure companies expect to attract new rich and/or high income target customer group to choose any one kind of space trip journey planning to consume.

These are indications that these types of customers are becoming interested in spending on an once-in-a-lifetime space experience. Therefore, the growth of the space tourism market is highly sensitive to customer satisfaction and how it is communicated through the various media. This will establish the status –factor of space tourism, and corresponding brand reputation of service providers. The minimum price goal for a variable space tourism business is currently estimate to be below US$3-4000/kg for a round-trip depending on vehicle configuration. So, space travel leisure companies need to concern every round space trip cost, it can depend on the space vehicle number and weight issue to influence every space trip ticket price variable to achieve how much it can earn.

On space journey design factor aspect, it includes these different facilities aspects how to design, because future space travelling consumers will concern whether the space travel company can provide special entertainment to satisfy their needs. The facilities include as below:

How to design space hotels to let them to live in comfortable space environment and eat the best taste and fresh food quality when the cookers need to cook in the space hotel in the space environment? How to design space swimming pools to let them to swim in safe space environment? How to design space sport centers to let them to run more easily in one space sport warm and safe environment? How to design one space garden to let them to see different species of Earth flowers, or plants? How to design one space farming land to let them to see different species of Earth fruits, vegetables, tomatoes, potatoes etc. fresh foods growth in warm and safe space farming land environment? How to design one space cinema to let them to watch movies in one safe and warm space cinema environment? All these facilities will be any one of future space trip's' important and attractive space trip leisure facilities to influence every space traveler to choose to buy the space tourism leisure company's space trip leisure service.

Instead of these space building entertainment facilities, they also need to concern how the space vehicle entertainment tools are provided the entertainment service to satisfy their needs. When the space travelers can sit on the space vehicles to move on any planets' lands, such as Moon. A number of space vehicle options exist in the market, mainly differing based on the seat capacity as well as the in-flight experience level offered. The typical space vehicle solution is a small, relatively light weight spacecraft taking between 2 to 10 passengers. The number of passengers depends on the service level, amenities and extra offered. The trip typically lasts about 10 hours and of which about 4 hours are spent in space. The main attraction is the weightless time after in space. The main attraction is the weightless time after re-entry has started. It is a rather low-G technology and therefore the medical requirements for participants are nor very high.

Consequently, the space vehicles, space leisure building facilities, the space trip reasonable price ticket level, every safe space trip journey arrangement, clean and fresh and good taste space food arrangement, space traveler individual real learning experience etc. these factors will be the main influential factors to raise the space tourism leisure company's competitive effort and the space traveler consumer individual consumption desire to the space tourism leisure company in the future.

Can COVID 19 disease influence Space travel marketing strategy changes?

Any space travel organization needs have good marketing strategy to prepare how to operate its space travelling leisure business in order to attract many space travelling clients to choose its space travelling service. I shall indicate these different strategies aspects whey they are needed to be concerned as below:

2.1 On concept of spacecraft design aspect

Firstly, on concept aspect, any one space travelling leisure company needs have at least one spacecraft to catch clients to fly to space to travel. So how to design the spacecraft and its quality and safety and comfortable environment spacecraft machine concept aspect issue which is one challenge to be concerned. Because many space travelling passengers ususally concern whether the spacecraft is safe, comfortable , good quality, as well as the space travelling leisure providers also need to concern whether the spacecraft is less time and energy saving efficient use, less manufactory operating cost and durable.

In general, space travelling leisure provider expects the spacecraft or spacecraft vehicle can be uesed long time. The spacecraft will be expected to utilize previous flight rated and proven technologies to from the basis for manufacturing spacecraft vehicles , and will incorporate the latest modern avionics and flight system for answering safety, reliability and economical operation.

In general, the spacecraft will be designed to carry two crew and approximately, 10,000 pounds of cargo, depending on the ultimate weight of the spacecraft. Relying on flight hardware to maintain the space station, such as Moon or Mar space station is fpr any space travelling spacecrafts to reach these space travelling destinations to stay, it is also need to consider by many space travelling experts as risky, extremely, expensive cost sensitive for any space station travelling destination design arrangement in order to future every spacecraft can fly to any planets to stay on its space station safely.

(1) Outsourcing spacecraft concept design strategy

As a result, outsourcing strategy is one good method to help them to reduce cost in order to achieve to let every space travel passenger has safe space journey experience and capacity for safely launching a fully loaded (including crew and cargo). Outsourcing strategy is the launch role to a major contracor, they can concentrate on crew flight training, planning all passnegers and cargo capacoty, and preparing flight manifests, and will as a result, avoid the expense of maintaining a launch operation on a daily basis. In addition, by outsoucing the spacecraft manufacturing, the space travelling provider can avoid spending millions of dollars on facilities and equipment infrastructure and engineering manufacturing expertise.

(2) On deciding misson aspect

Secondly, on mission aspect, any space travelling journey needs have a clear mission to be planned how to achieve in order to ensure every space travelling passenger feel satisfactory in the space travelling journey. So, every whole space travelling journey arrangement, e.g. where will be the space travelling destination, how to check every space travelling planned passengers' bodies whether who are health to catch spacecraft to fly to space to travel or how to train every space travelling planned passenger to ensure whom can permit to catch spacecraft to fly to space to travel, how to arrange every space travelling journey entertainment and facilities to let either young or old age target passenger to enjoy the space trip to feel satisfactory, how to arrange different days of every space trip.

In the last few years, Virgin Galactic has been making new's headlines with its promises to provide space travel services, and announcement that it will soom offer, at quite a hefty price, trips to sub-orbit. It is generally agreed that sub-orbit exists 100 kilometres above the earth's sea-level (Von Der Dunk, 2012). Hence, Virgin Galactic will provide travel to where customers may experience weightlessness, as well as the sight of earth's curvature. Even more interesting is that Virgin Galactic is not the only company with such a mission,there are a few more that wish to offer the same type of service. For example, some companies even aim to provide an orbital type of flight.

Orbit flight suggests that humans would venture into outer space, where they might either orbit the earth or board the international space station (hereinafter: ISS). In addition, some envision space hotels, moon visitations and mining asteroids. Although at first such statement might seem for one must point out that a "space hotel" is already in earth's orbit and that diligent progress through flight tests is almost made the commercial aspect of regular space travel a reality; it is only the question of time and readiness for the companies to make their long-awaited and open a new industry of present day economics (Klemm & Markkanen, 2011; Berry , 2012).

So, every space travelling mission is to ensure that reliable, technologically-sophisicated competitively-priced flight certified spacecraft are designed and properly maintained when performing their every assigned space travelling journey mission. The space traveller leisure provider will need to provide a carefully selected array of techologies that are capable of meeting the requirements of travelling into earth orbit. It will emphasize affordability, reliability, safety, customer service and responsiveness in responding to customer's space travelling requirements.

For this space tourism leisure mission example, it many include these objectives , such as below:

One trip into space, sending a space vehicle of a certain make and with a specify capacity on a space mission, provides the various grades of a core service, such as a space mission including issues such as waiting and delivery times, personal attention and advice, amenities and facilities, ensure quality assurance, it is the planned and system activities implemented in a quality system. So that quality requirements for a product or service will be fulfilled. It aims at preventing high-risk adverse events, or reducing thei impact, provides excellent customer satisfaction, it is a measure of how products and services meet the space travelling customer expectations, customer satisfaction is also always evaluated in relationship of every space travelling ticket price of the space travelling entertainment service and spacecraft product comfortable environment feeling and good leisure arrangement for every space travelling leisure journey.

(3) On space tourism leisure organization managment aspect

Thirdly, on space tourism leisure organization management aspect, it is also important to influence efficient and excellent space service performance to be provided to satisfy every space travel organization management team needs to be consists of experienced professionals who have successfully management and operated companies specializing in the aerospace industry for a number of years.

Their knowledge and contacts within the space industry will prove invaluable in assisting the space tourism leisure provider in the achievement of its goals and objectives. In individuals on the team components that up a spacecraft tourism development organization, and have unique experience in the design, construction, operations and maintenance of the major functions will developing spacecraft for launching into orbit. Every spacecraft will be built and maintained utilizing the same high standards of quality, within budget and well within time constraints.

Hence, every space tourism provider needs have one excellent management leaders to manage every space tourism service staffs to serve passengers in order to achieve excellent service performance to let them every one to feel satisfactory, during their every space tourism journey (trip).

(4) On target audience prediction aspect

On target audience prediction aspect, every space trip needs have identifies target travelling passenger in order to concentrate to choose the most popular and satisfactory space travelling journey for their identified needs.

For primary audiences example, it can include space enthusiasts and educational families both. Space enthusiasts target are usually young people and they are only 20% over 65 age old people target space ethusiasts who will be the future potential space tourism target consumers as well as the educational families target who will aspect owning educational experience for children , who is the explicit reason to visit space, either he/she has interest in history of space exploration or he/she has interest in future of space exploration or he/she feels that spce trip looked like fun.

KSCVC Visots (2013) indicated that future top markets, ranked by high visitation against space enthusiasts and educational families space tourism passengers, the US cities will include: Orlando, NYC, Miami, Tampa Bay, Chicago, West plam, Philadelphia, Atlanta, Boston, Washington, DC and San Francisco cities. So, future US space travelling market will be the top one in the world.

(5) On space objective aspect

On space objective aspect, instead of any one space tourism leisure organization concerns how to achieve its mission to satisfy all space tourism passengers leisure needs. Although, it is the major missin for space tourism leisure industry. But they can not neglect what the objectives are in order to develop or achieve long term space tourism leisure missions more easily. The objectives main open space key issues can include such as: Providing an adequate supply of land to meet the future needs of strategic opn space links, natural areas and recreational facilities on any future space tourism destinations, increasing pressure for public access to open space areas with conservation values, competing interests between adjoining land use and development on public open space and its user groups, use of public open space and recreational resources for drainage purposes, raising higher space traveller hotel residential development placing increased pressure on the demand for public open space planet land use aim and developing public open space mor intensive leisure and sport activities on any future new space tourism planet destinations.

When the space tourism leisure providers have long term objectives to attempt to solve above these any one of key issues. It will ahve a more clear objective to achieve its long term space tourism leisure business market. It's long term objectives can include such as below:

To identify existing and future active and passive recreation needs and social trends of future space tourism visitors; to provide a wide range of high quality and accessible public open space public land areas to encourage physical activity and social interaction to meet the existing and future needs of space travelling visitors; to identify existing gaps in the public open space network and develop any different kinds of space trip arrangement to satisfy the different identified target space traveller individual needs; to protect enhance and increase landcrapt values of public open space land use; to recognize the hierarchy of public open space assets; equitably distributing open space resources; access to facilities and a diverse range of opportunities to incorporate the drainage function in public open space travelling destination areas without detriment to safely, environmental, visual and recreational values.

So, these development of any space planets howo to use their lands objectives will bring long term space travelling destination beneficial advantages to raise to build the space hotels, space swimming pools, space gardens, space cinemas, space sport places to let future space travelers can

stay in Mars or Moon planet destinations to enjoy these leisure facilities and they can feel which are similar to our earth leisure facilities attractively.
These space buildings are important to attract future space travellers to catch spacecraft to fly to Mars or Moon planet to travel in possible because it is fun and exciting space trip when these leisure facilities can be built on Moon or Mars to let space travellers to stay short days in either these two planets to live their space hotels. So how to build any one of these space leisure building which is another important objective for any future space tourism leisure business, instead of how to arrange any space destination trip objective. So, any space tourism leisure provider ought not neglect how to achieve these two main space tourism objectives.
However, these are key questions continually asked regarding the viability of space tourism. They concern financial, marketing and political communities. Their concerns can be best addredded in a properly, comprehensive business plan. Some questions can not be answered definitively at this time. Hoever, knowledge of the concerns and developing space businesses in any space traveling leisure planning stages and efforts to raise capital in the following questions, every spce tourism leisure business leader needs to concern this questions as below:
Can the space tourism industry into a profitable enonomic industry?
Are challenges related to financing, marketing, business methodologies or a combination of all of these facets?
Can the proponents of space tourism to be proven business tools and methodologies in their presentation of an acceptable business plan?
Can at least a cost effective, certified passenger space tourism journey to be developed for space tourism?
What effects will influence space-tourism businesses of NASA begins selling seats on the US space shuttle to civilian space tourists?
All above questions will be every new space tourism leisure businessman who needs to concern questions in order to achieve whose marketing strategy more successfully. Consequently, marketing strategy is important to be prepared in order to follow corrective steps to achieve every space tourism leisure business missions and objectives more easily.

2.2 Space tourism leisure behavioral economic consumption model

In space tourism leisure industry, due to every time space trip needs the space travelling planner to plan how much budget to consume expensive spce ticket price. So, it seems that the target customers will be rich or high income level young people or the retirement rich old people target customer group.

So, it brings this question: How to persuade these rich or high income young people or rich retirement old people to prefer to spend spce tourism leisure at least one time in their life?

It is one valuabe research question to every future space tourism leisure provider. I shall indicate the successful factors to analyze how to persuade them to accept this kind of potential space travelling leisure in behavioral economic personal consumption view point, in order to explain the cause and effect relationship between of these factors as below:

(1) Economic environment variable factor

Firstly, it is economic environment variable factor whether it can influence to space tourism leisure consumption changing. As I discuss about economic environment variable issue will influence consumption behavior changing. For space tourism leisure case, it is not now kind of essential consumption leisure product to every one. So , even the rich or high income people who will be influences to seek this kind of leisure to play, it the economic environment is improved, it will influence they have positive attitude and interest to choose this kind of leisure consumption. However, if the economic environment is worse, it will influence they have negative attitude and no interest to choose this kind of leisure consumption, due to space travel is one kind of expensive leisure consumption to every one.

Hence, in this space tourism leisure industry, it does not ensure that the rich or high income people must be persuade to choose this kind of expensive space tourism entertainment in whose holiday or retirement time. They can have the common tourism entertainment to go to different countries to travel many times in our earth. Otherwise, space tourism leisure is more expensive to compare common earth tourism leisure , it means that the rich or high income people only spend one time spacecraft catching to fly to space to travel in their life, it is more difficult to every space traveler like to catch spacecraft to fly to space to travel more than one time, due to he/she had attempted to catch spacecraft to fly to space to travel to own space travel experience, he/she will feel enough satisfactory and enjoyment in common. Hence, it is possible that future many rich or high income people only like to spend one time space tourism leisure, then they won't continue to spend this kind of tourism entertainment again in their life.

Thus, space tourism leisure providers need to arrange any special or attractive space tourism leisure to persuade these high income or rich target clients to consume, when the economic environment will change worse. The Europen space agency (ESA), defines this phenomenon between economic environment variable and space tourism client growth or falling number relationship as: " space tourism is an execution of sub-orbital flight by privately finded and/or privately operated vehicles and the technology development driven by space tourism market."

it seems that space vehicle is one attractive travelling desire tool will be one attractive selling point to influence space tourism leisure consumer individual entertainment choice or attitude to be changed to positive leisure consumption attitude to prefer to play this kind of space tourism activities when economic environment changes to worse. Hence, when economic environment is worse, the economic wore changing factor will influence the space travelling planner individual leisure consumption desire, even it will influence the rich or high income young people or rich retirement people target customer both groups.

As (ESA, 2008) indicated space vehicle will be one kind of attractive leisure tool for spce traveler. So, I suggest that space tourism lesiure journey arrangement needs to include that such as : the space travelers can catch space vehicle to move on Moon or Mars plants land to feel what the different feeling is between during they are catching public transportation tool, such as bus or taxi during the are catching these transportation tools on earth land and during they are catching space vehicle tools on Mars or Moon planet's lands. It is so exicting and fun catching space vehicle tool experience on these both Mars or Moon planets‘ lands to the young and old age space travelling passengers. Because every space vehicle's speed is not very fast and it will move on Moon or Mars planets slowly. So, any aged pace travelling passengers can attempt to play this kind of space facilities leisure after they catched spacecraft to fly to these both Mars or Moon planet to stay. They can spend half hour or one hour, even more than one hour to catch the space vehicle to go to anywhere on Mars or Moon to travel. It is possible that they can find exciting and undiscovered things on these both planets.

So, catching space vehicle to go to anywhere on either these both planets journey, it will one essential part of space travelling journey during the economic environment is changed to worse. It is extra attractive space travelling leisure journey to attract space tourism consumer individual leisure desire when economic environment is worse.

Hence, from this perspective then space tourism could be understood as a section of the tourism industry mainly based on technological development, progression and its activitity being related specifically to sub orbital flights. So, if future space tourism providers expect whether the global economic environment changing will be better or worse which won't influence space tourism leisure consumption desire to be changed. The space tourism leisure providers need to persuade the space tourism planners feel space tourism would have to be treated like an already exciting part of the tourism industry. It means that space tourism leisure is one kind of tourism leisure choice to replace common earth tourism leisure consumption. When travelers feel space tourism is another tourism leisure to replace which can replace common earth tourism leisure. It will avoid the worse economic environment changing factor to reduce the rich or high income young people or rich retirement old people whose space travelling leisure consumption desire.

Consequently , the question in relation to, in what kinds of space tourism journey message do space travel providers promote behind whether space vehicle journey promotion message which is needed when economic environment will change worse. I shall be asked, as understanding the meaning in which space tourism is being marketed, communicated is seen as a factor , which can either positively contribute to future development of the tourism industry or lead into prolonging or seen stopping the space tourism industry from its progression.

(2) Space tourism leisure journey management factor

Secondly, space tourism leisure jounrey management factor, how to arrange every space tourism leisure journey which will be one important factor to influence space tourism planner individual tourism consumption desire.

In general, it can includes these several forms of space tourism leisure activities in every space lesiure trip arrangement. The following classification of space tourism include: Terrestria spce tourism (i.e. NASA visit centre, space movies, online space experience); Atmospheric space tourism (i.e. : MIG 31 flight, zero G. flights) and astro (orbita) tourism (i.e.: trips to the international space station-beyond earth orbit) (Cater 2010, Crouch et al. 2009).

Instead of US domestic space tourism market is potential, next country is Japan. First, the study is made by Collins et. al (1994, 1996) in Japan on 3030 research participants, showed that 80% of respondents under the age of 50 were willing to travel to space and out of them 20% were willing to pay year's salary for the space travel experience. Yet, it could be citicized that the Japan people age group of under 50 could be too broad, in general different generations under one groups. nest besides the willingness to go to space, the Japanese study showed respondents motivations for travelling to space, including any fun and exciting attractive space tourism journey, e.g. interest in space walk, catching space vehicle or driving space vehicle on the either Moon or Mars planets, earth view, zeo gravity experience, livin gin space hotels one night or more, watching movies in space cinemas, swimming in space pools, visiting space gardens, running in space sport centers, catching spacecrafts to view earth or Moon or Mars planets.

Hence, it seems attractive space tourism journey can persuade another country's space travelling planners, such as Japanese attempts to satisfy whose space tourism needs. So, different kinds of attractive space trip journey arrangement will be one important factor to influence young and old age travelling consumption desire. It implies that attractive space tourism journey will be one influential factor to encourage other countries tourism consumers attempt to another kind of leaving earth tourism leisure. So, any space tourism trip destinations and leisure facilities arrangement must need to satisfy space traveler individual leisure needs and every space trip must be more fun, exciting and comfortable and enjoyable feeling to compare general tourism journey in earth. Due to general earth tourism leisure will be space tourism leisure's competitive or replaced leisure product and service. Hence, space trip destinations and leisure facilities choice will be one important factor to influence space travelling planner's consumption desire.

Every space travelling planner will compare general earth travelling leisure's destinations and leisure facilities arrangement whether the space travelling trip arrangement , leisure facilities arrangement and food arrangement, space vehicle or spacecraf leisure comfortable influence issues which will have more satisfactory enjoyable feeling to compare general earth tourism leisure and their spending expenditure to every space trip whether is value or is not value.

Consequently, economic environment changing factor and space trip and leisure facilities arrangement factor which both will influence any space tourism planner individual consumption desire mainly. So, space tourism businessmen ought concern these two aspects of factors how and when will change to adapt any country's potential space traveler's space tourism changing taste and needs in order to follow the new space tourism changing needs easily.

Space tourism market moral ethic risk

threats

What are space tourism moral ethic risk during the space businessmen operate this businesses as well as what market threats who will encounter to face difficulties ? I shall give actul cases to explain how and why these challenges will cause to influence any new space tourism businesses development successfully.

(1) Potential accidents aspect

Firstly, space travelers will concern that public reactions to potential accidents aspect during they are catching spacecrafts to travel to space. In fact, it is moral ethic responsibility to any space tourism leisure providers to provide safe, comfortable and non accident occurrence in their whole space trip. Because once time accident will cause any one of space passenger hurt or death. So , it must be any space tourism businessmen responsibilities to concern whether they have enough confidence to ensure none any accident occurrences in every space tourism trip.

Hence, in space tourism industry, government needs have public policy to threaten or prohibit any space tourism leisure providers neglect to often check and ensure any spacecraft machines or equipments are regular opeations, as well as often renew new spacecraft machines when they are old to be used. The policy is a force effort to need them to abide every space tourism leisure safe responsibility to ensure or guarantee any one of spacecraft won't have accident occurrences during it has left earth to fly to space in whole space trip journey from the beginning to the end till to the spacecraft come to earth safely.

Hence, this policy forces any space tourism leisure providers concern to put a monetary value on increased or reduced risk of death, the " value of statistical live", used to characterize when the benefit of safety regulation is worth the cost such regulation improves. So, the country government and the country's space tourism leisure providers both have responsibilities to guarantee all space tourism passengers' life safety. It must not allow any death or hurt occurrences during every space tourism trip.

Even, the country government can have legal action to publish any space tourism leisure providers, when their every space tourism trip has occurred accidents, e.g. fire accident occurrence in spacecarft or spacecrat machines are broken to be damaged and need to be repaired during the space tourism trip. It will threaten to reduce trip accident occurrence, such as this cases. The commercial space ventures may present risk to property as well, such as a fire starting on the ground by launch-related material or problems presented by space debris.

In principle, liability law can provide incentive to deter carelessness that could lead to the destruction of property, although statutory (rather than common law) assignments of liability for commercial launches are somewhat problematic.

Consequently, if the space tourism leisure provider expected to grow space tourism passenger number in long -term time, it must need to ensure none any accidents can occur during any space trip. Otherwise, the space tourism passengers can choose another space tourism leisure provider to replace its spce tourism leisure easily.

(2) Space tourism destinations and space tourism entertainment facilities safe arrangement challenges aspect

Secondly, it is space tourism destinations and space tourism entertainment facilities safe arrangement challenges. Nowadays, commercial space travel is looking more like a real possibility than science fiction. The usual ethical issues related to the safety of the space destination choices and the space tourism entertainment facilities, e.g. space vehicles, space hotels, space swimming pools, space sport centers, space cinemas, space gardens, space farming lands. In this strange space environment and safety concerns are just the beginning as there are othe interesting questions, such as below:

What likely would be a fair process for commercializing or claiming property in any space planets? Such as Moon or mars, when any future space tourism leisure providers who need to build above these any one of space entertainment facilities on these planets to provide to their space travelling customers to play.

How to distribute and manage these any lands ownership to these future space tourism providers fairly and legally?

How likely would a separatist movement be among space settlements to want to be free and independent states?

How to ensure above future space entertainment facilities and space entertainment places are in the safe space environment to be provided to any space travelers to play in any planets, e.g. Moon or Mars etc. planets.

So, concerning how to arrange space entertainment facilities to provide to space tourism clients to play in any safe space environment issue, it will be another concerning question to every space tourism leisure providers. When they decide to choose anywhere to the space hotels, space swimming pools, space gardens, space cinemas or space farming lands or space sport centers. These space buildings will need to be built in the safe, on stable stone lands environment and none any natural distaster, such as large wind or space underground water etc. unpredictable space natural distasterr attack to these space buildings suddenly. Because it has responsibility to any space tourism leisure providers to guarantee any one of these space buildings are safe to be built in the planet's safe land environment. It aims to achieve none any accident occurrences during their space tourism clients are staying to enter these any one of space buildings to visit or play any space entertainment facilities safely, e.g. space vehicle.

So, they must need to ceck anywhere the space planet's places to be ensured safe to build any buildings. Then, they can choose the suitable locations to build space entertainment facilities or buildings more confidently.

In fact, any space entertainment facilities, e.g. space hotels, space farming lands as well as space transportation tools, e.g. spce vehicle, spacecraft , these things will be value to be concerned to any space tourism leisure providers and it is business moral ethic responsibility to every one of them, when they plan to develop their space tourism business in any planets.

(3) Space tourism market competition challenge aspect

Thirdly, any provate space tourism development leisure businesses will face market competitive challenge, such as large spacefaring countries, e.g. US, UK have possible to dominate future space tourism leisure business (government can own space tourism leisure business). They will be main actors in space were nation-states. Large spacefaring counties can build the space vehicles, that can take people and cargo into orbit and to the Moon, or Mars crafted international space law and shaped the main investments in space tourism leisure technology.

So, it is possible that the own space technological developed countries, such as US, UK, these countries governemts will have possible to operate public fund to support space tourism leisure business. It implies that private space tourism leisure businesses will face public space tourism leisure business and themselve private space tourism leisure business market competition in space tourism leisure industry.

If these two countries governments also participate this private space tourism leisure market. It will raise market threats to any private space tourism organizations.

Whether will developed countries governments participate private space tourism market? It is possible that new commercial actors began to enter the space tourism leisure industry, looking to disrupt both space launch services ans use space in new exotic ways. For example, the US government also moved its purposeful degradatoin of the global positioning system (GPS), so US government will have effort to dominate GPS global positioning system communication business also. As this GPS communication business case, future US government has possible to decide to participate space tourism leisure business also.

However, in the future, space tourism leisure industry may contribute even more the developed countries, e.g. American, England economy. Space tourism and resource recovery, e.g. mining on planet, Moons and asteroids in particular may become large parts of that space tourism industry if these countries governments participated to this space tourism industry development. Of course, their viability rests on a range of factors, including costs , future regulation, international market competivitive problems and assumption about space technological development. However, these is increasing optimism in these areas of economic production to bring human space tourism leisure enjoyment and space mining resource development benefits. But the space economy is not just about what happens in orbits or how that alters life on the ground. The growth of this economy can also contribite to new innovations across all future possible unpredictable or undiscovered technological development, instead of space tourism leisure or space mining resource exploitation development.

Consequently, any space development technological governments will have possible to bring economic benefits from either only private space tourism leisure organizations or governments and private space tourism leisure both organizations cooperate to participate to achieve space tourism misson to contribute to global economic development and create new jobs to be employed in space labor supply market.

3.1 Can space tourism business bring economy benefits

It is fact that space tourism activities have a positive and beneficial impact on eveyday life and society and this help space travelers to understand that, despite the high space ticket prices of any space tourism leisure choices. However, space tourism will bring scientific knowledge and technological knowhow and jobs to bring humn tangible or untangible both benefits. I shall indicate these benefits as below:

Although, space tourism leisure seems only leisure activities to be consumed to satisfy any space tourism individual travelling need. However, it can assign space scientists to research and attempt discovery these intangible benefits: Such as tele-communications revolution, satellite weather forecasting, mapping mineral exploration, water resource management diaster mitigation, national security or other undiscovered untangible benefits. Because every spacecraft needs to plan to fly to space, and it will reach any space planet stations, e.g. Mars, Moon planet when it visits these any one planet, the space scientists can attempt to find new undiscovered space resource , e.g. mining or finding new undiscovered satellite weather forecasting method when they can reach these planets to attempt to do space scientifical investigtion to research new space resource , or find any space stones attack to our methods to avoid earth disaster occurrence (national security mission), instead of the spacecraft catchs space passengers to visit these planets to enjoy these planets space entertainment facilities in their space trip journeys.

(1) On space resource benefit aspect

Hence, the space tourism intangible benefits include: space exploration and international cooperation is developing sophisticted space technologies by nations. For example, the images of distant stars and glaxies using Hubble telescope, research laboratory such as international space station to conduct experiments in biology, human biology, physics, Astronomy and meteorology under microgravity environment and testing of the spacecraft systems will be required for space tourism missions to the Moon and Mars. In the future, human would be able to have unlimited and clean solar energy from space for our industries as well as heating and lighting our homes. In the near future , it would be possible to disposed-off our nuclear waste safely and unexpensively and released towards the sun using a space elevator. We many become a space tourist in earth orbit or on the Moon or Mars. We may carry and extra-terrestial mining and even introduce the development of a multi-planet economy.

(2) On education benefit aspect

Another on education benefit aspect, space tourism can let space travelers to feel actual space learning experiences, during the spacecraft is flying in the space. Their space environment learning experience can include, for example: How many spacecraft have been launched by a given country? How many phone calls are made over a satellite? How many lives could be saved by resue satellites? How they feel differences when they are living in one space hotels, they are swimming in the swimming pools, they are visiting the space garden, they are running in one space sport centers, they are visiting in one space farming land, they are sitting or driving one space vehicle on planet land, or they are catching one spacecraft.

These space learning experience will let they feel what the actual differences between space environment and earth environment. It is one humankind learning experience education service in any space planet's Moon or Mars remote areas, bringing information and tourism entertainment facilities to the masses. The space experience learning knowledge can provide data to let these space travelers to know, such as how ships can be safe at sea, monitoring the threat of pollution, how enhancing durable medical instruments for better health-care enabling hikers and skiers to be located when lost, many more. So, it seems space tourism can bring much positive benefits as no negative impact on space activitied has been found by the society , the investments are made by the nations on space activites are justified and not the waste of money.

● What are the tangible social and economic benefits brought from space tourism?

In most advanced economies space tourism or space resource exploitation industry is seen as an enabler that improves lives and helps to develop both economic and social spheres. Space industry economic can include these aspect: Application of space technology to space tourism navigation, meteorological forcasting and broadcast of on live television and internet connectivity to lesser-known applications, such as precision agriculture, transport, tracking, resource extraction and monitoring of utility networks.

Additional application exists in the disaster monitoring and relif, insurance and military applications. Thus, data coming from satellites is important to all economic sectors, making the world a better and safer place.

International space tourism experience would suggest that space travelling leisure businesses deliver value by providing a central point for academia industry , defence and foreign entities to collaborate among themselves and with government and to facilitate the flow of knowledge and capital.

How can space tourism industry maximize the socio-economic benefits?

In fact, our growing use of space derived data and systems is our growing dependence on a better and safer sapce planet, e.g. Moon or Mars and to provide space tourism safe services that space travelling service that space traveler all benefit from industry in telecommunication , health, transport , banking , security and climate change monitoring.

The space tourism positive influence result is long term, the positive contribution to our quality of life is real. In other word, the world for space tourism leisure activities is changing the internationally space tourism sector is experiencing a profound revolution.

In conclusion, space tourism leisure countries with historical leadership in space tourism have been under positive as a result of a tough financial environment leading to the definition of their space travelling technology priorities. In the meantime, new space entertainment travelling leaders, such as US, UK , even China, India have ambitions in space tourism through massive investments in the development of their capabilities in space travelling leisure business aspect.

So, the future space travelling entertainment market is large, due to China and India both have many rich people and high income people, who expect to consume in space tourism leisure trip at least one time in their lifes. Consequently, worldwide space tourism entertainment industry players are rethinking their busines models and strategies as they experience discuptive innovations, competitive space tourism entertainment and new drivers impacting the spacecraft and any space entertainment facilities manufacturing on Moon or Mars planet, launch and space tourism entertainment related businesses. Thus, we can in fact in talk about a new space tourism business, in which more and more innovative applications of space tourism data are developed dependence on space tourism data in everyday life rises and increasing share of economic growth relies on the space tourism market both in terms of opportunity benefits , e.g. India and China spce tourism potential market development and any concern space tourism job creation to every countries. Hence, space tourism development can bring positive economic benefits to any countries.

Reference

Cater Iain , Carl 2010, " Steps to space: Opportunities for astro tourism development, tourism management 31 (2010); pp. 838-845; Elsevier Ltd, DOI: 10:1016/j.tourman. 2009.09.001

Collins Patric, Iwasaki Yoichi, Kanayama Hideki, Ohnuki Misuzo 1994, comercial implications of market research on space tourism. journal space technology and sciences , vol. 10 no 2, 94 Autumn, pp.3-11. copyright: Japanese rocket society; available at: www.spacefuture.com/archive/ commercial-implications-of market-research-on-space- tourism.shtml.

Collins Patric, Marita M; Stockmans R. and Kobayahi S. 1996. "Demand for space tourism in America and Japan and its implications for future space activities ". sixth international space conference of Pacific basic societies; Marina del rey; California: Advantages in the Astronautica science (AAS paper no AAS 95-605) vol. 91. pp. 601-610. Available at:
http://m.internationalaerospaceconsulting.org/upload/space % 20Future% 20-%20Demand% 20for%20space% 20Tourism%20in% 20America%20Japan.pdf

ESA 2008, " Richard Garriott, millionaire American space tourist. blasks off of international space station". published in 12.11.2008. Huffington post, seen on i01.04.2015; available at: http://www.huffington.com/2008/10/ 12/richard-garriott-milliona-n-1333940.html.

Klemm, G., & Markkanen, S. (2011). IN A Papathanassis (ed.) The long Tai , tourism (pp.95-103). Weisbaden, Germany : Gabler Verlag; Springer Fachmedien Weiesbaden GmbH.

KSCVC Visitors, 2013; MRI 2013 Market by Market

Von Der Dunk , F. (2012). The integrated approach. Regulating private human spaceflight as space activity, aircraft operation, and high-risk adventure tourism. Acta Astronautica, 92(2), 199-208.

Future space tourism psychology
prediction stragegy

- Psychology and economic environment changing both factors influence whole space tourism market leisure desire

How can psychology method predict space tourism leisure desire? I believe that it has relationship between the space tourism planner and the economic environment as well as his/her psychology as below:
Firstly, on the economic environment influence hand, it includs these both economic situations, either in the good economic environment, many people can earn high income and employers can supply many job number to provide to many people to work, then it will influence the space travelling planner has more space travelling desire. Otherwise, or in the bad economic, less people can earn high income and employers can not supply

many job number to provide to many people to work, it will influence the space travelling planner has less space travelling desire.

Secondly, on these both the space travelling planner individual psychology influence hand, the space travelling planner will have these both aspects of individual psychological influence, it includes these both either positive or negative psychological influence aspectsas below:

On the positive psychological influence aspect, if the space travelling planner has confidence to the space travelling leisure company can provide safe, comfortable, good quality of one space travelling trip arrangement, good taste food arrangement, reasonable space ticket price and every reasonable space trip for space hotel living arrangement and space garden and space farming land visiting journey arrangement, even, space swimming pool and space sport centre and space cinema leisure arrangement to let whom to stay on the planet at least one day trip, it means not one short time space trip, e.g. the spacecraft only flies about half hour or one half. It can not fly to the planet to arrive its space station destination to stay to let the space travelling planner to live at the space hotel at least one night. Then the space travelling planner will have more desire to choose to catch the space tourism leisure company's spacecraft to travel to space.

Otherwise, on the negative psychological influence aspect, if the space travelling planner lacks confidence to the space travelling leisure company can provide safe, comfortable, good quality of one space travelling trip arrangement, good taste food arrangement, reasonable space ticket price and every reasonable space trip for space hotel living arrangement and space garden and space farming land visiting journey arrangement, even, space swimming pool and space sport centre and space cinema leisure arrangement to let whom to stay on the planet at least one day trip, it means not one short time space trip, e.g. the spacecraft only flies about half hour or one half. It can not fly to the planet to arrive its space station destination to stay to let the space travelling planner to live at the space hotel at least one night. Then the space travelling planner will have less desire to choose to catch the space tourism leisure company's spacecraft to travel to space.

Hence, it seems economic environment changing factor and the space travelling planner's confidence factor to the space tourism leisure providers will influence the whole space travelling market whose space travelling consumer's space travelling leisure consumption desire to be more or less. So, any one space tourism provider can not neglect these both factors how to influence whose customer consumption desire.

- space tourism strategy

Future any space tourism leisure business needs have good business plan to outline the space tourism leisure business in these aspects , such as: different space tourism destinations of every space tourism journey, technical , financial and regulatory factors for growing space tourism leisure consumption into any one kind of unique artificial intelligent space tourism journey for identified passenger target group.

All how to design one space tourism business development plan to attempt to predict whether what trends will influence how every different kinds of identified space tourism journey in order to achieve passenger number growing aim as well as how to achieve one attractive space tourism leisure to satisfy future space tourism passenger individual space travel needs more easily.

I shall indicate what aspects to future every space tourism traveler who will consider in order to reduce the space tourism traveler personal worry to catch any pace boats to leave our Earth to fly to other planets to travel.

I recommend that any space tourism leisure organizations need to concern these aspects in their space tourism leisure business plan as below:

(1) safe space tourism journey

On first aspect concerns safe space tourism journey plan to let all space tourism travelers will considerate safe issue. They must ensure space boats that is safe to catch them to fly to planets in their space journeys. So, any space tourism leisure business will utilize previous flight rated and proven technologies to form the basis for manufacturing spacecraft vehicles, and will incorporate the latest modern avionics and flight systems for ensuring safety, reliability and economical operation in order to reduce any space tourism traveler personal worry to catch any spacecraft.

So, the space tourism safe journey plan is one very important factor to influence space tourism consumer number for them if any one of space tourism leisure business hoped they can grow the space tourism consumer number for long term. For example, the space boat flight hardware must often be maintained at the space station. It is needed to be considered by space boat experts as risky, extremely expensive and potentially sensitive. To aims to ensure spacecraft will offer an economical and safe alternative for any satellite manufacturers and other space tourism entertainment organizations have a desire or requirement for space tourism flight.

(2) reduction cost expense plan
On second aspect concerns reduction cost expense plan, any space tourism entertainment organizations need have the experience and capacity for safely launching a fully loaded , including space tourism passengers and passenger individual cargo for every spacecraft tourism journey. As a result of outsourcing the launch role to a major contractor, the space tourism pilot can concentrate on space boat crews flight training, planning space tourism passenger cargo capacity and preparing space flight manifests , and will as a result, avoid the expense of maintaining a launch operation on a daily basis. In addition, by outsourcing the spacecraft manufacturing, it can avoid spending millions of dollar on facilities and equipment infrastructure and engineering manufacturing expertise.

(3) achieve any space tourism mission plan
On third aspect concerns how to achieve any space tourism mission. Every space tourism mission must be ensure that reliable service is provided to satisfy every space tourism passenger personal space traveler needs and let them to enjoy in their whole space tourism journey, let them to catch a big aircraft in comfortable environment of technologically sophisticated space boat, reasonable and competitive every time space tourism flight ticket price plan is developed and properly revised every time space tourism ticket price when performing their assigned every different space tourism journey mission.
Hence, the space tourism leisure company will provide one careful selected space tourism destination , e.g. Mar planet space tourism journey, Moon planet space tourism journey or no any space destination journey, it means that the space craft only needs to fly one circle around between Earth and Moon space journey etc. that are capable of meeting the requirements of travelling into Earth orbit. So, any space tourism journey must emphasize affordability, reliability, safety, customer service and responsiveness in responding to every client's space tourism journey requirements. Hence, any one of space tourism journey must have clear space journey mission and objective to satisfy any space traveler client target needs.

Methods to raise space
traveler number

Future space tourism will be one kind of new travel leisure market for any new space travel leisure companies to enter this undiscovered market in the beginning. However, how to predict future 10 to 20 years , even more space traveler number that is one important issue to any new space tourism leisure companies.

I think that space tourism leisure companies need to define what kinds of space travel leisure service to be provided to space travelling passengers, however, what age group of space passengers who will be their space travelling target client. For example, their space travel leisure must provide any flight operation that takes one or more passengers beyond the altitude of 100 km and thus into space to let space travelling passengers who have fun, exciting space travelling feeling.

Anyway, for any kind of space tourism (leisure space travel) journey, space tourism leisure company needs anyone to be bring customer satisfaction, it is a plan or predictive methods to measure how to let every space travelling passenger to feel comfortable when they are catching the spacecraft (space flying product) and they can have enjoyable and fun or exciting feeling when they have need providing any space tourism journey, services meet or surpass customer expectations.

Thus, any space tourism leisure company needs to evaluate the degree of every time space tourism journey's customer satisfaction and customer satisfaction is also always evaluated in relationship to the every time ticket price of the space tourism journey. So, the space tourism leisure company will predict the next time of what the space tourism journey of passenger number is more accurate, after it has evaluated what degree of every time space tourism journey's customer satisfaction is. It aims to gather their opinions to find which aspects that they need to revise, e.g. choosing where will be the next time space tourism journey destination, how to improve spacecraft staff's service attitude and performance to serve to their space tourism passengers when they are catching the spacecraft, to evaluate whether the spacecraft can provide comfortable and safe environment to let them to catch in order to let the next time space travelling passengers can feel satisfactory and enjoyable when they are catching the space tourism leisure's spacecraft to fly to anywhere in space.

In general, the expectation of factors space passengers include the following customer value elements, such as below:

- viewing space and the Earth.
- experiencing weightlessness and being able to float freely in zero gravity.

- experiencing pre-flight astronaut training and related sensations.
- communicating from space to significant others.
- being able to discuss the adventure in an informed way.
- having astronaut like documentation and memorabilia.

These objectives need to be combined with, sometimes conflicting constraints, such as guaranteed safe return, limited training time, reasonable comfort, and minimum medical restrictions. All these above issues which will be every space travelling passenger considerate matters before they choose the space tourism leisure company to catch its spacecraft to fly to space. So, all these factors will influence the next time space passenger number. Any space tourism leisure company can not neglect how to solve these all matters before they decide when their next time space tourism journey to be achieved.

Consequently, if the space craft tourism leisure company could revise what aspects of its last space tourism journey to find what are its wrong or weakness or unattractive challenges to cause any one space travelling passenger who feels unsatisfactory. Then, it can have more effort to concentrate on improving its next space tourism journey to raise its space tourism service performance level , e.g. people, food, leisure etc. service aspects and its space tourism product quality level, e.g. proving comfortable spacecraft facilities to let space travelling passengers to catch in whole spacecraft tourism journey. Then, it will have more confidence to achieve the raising space travelling passenger number.

- What is the prediction space travelling passenger desire method ?

The prediction space travelling passenger individual desire method can be one survey investigation method. When every time spacecraft finishes space tourism journey mission, after all space tourism passengers catch the spacecraft to arrive earth from space. When they arrive earth space station destination, then the space tourism leisure company can arrange survey investigation staffs to enquire their feeling for this time space tourism journey immediately.

The survey content can include as below:

Do you feel satisfactory or unsatisfactory to which aspects of this time space tourism journey?

(1) On service aspect questions include as below:

(a) Do you feel space food taste is good?

(b) Do you enjoy this time space tourism journey arrangement?

(c) Do you feel satisfactory to space staff
service performance?
(d) If you have unsatisfactory feeling for any one of above questions, which aspect issue cause you feel unsatisfactory to explain to let us to know in order to us to revise our service performance.

(2) On product aspect questions include as below:
(a) Do you feel comfortable when you are catching our spacecraft in whole space tourism journey?
(b) If you feel comfortable , may you explain the reasons what aspects of our spacecraft has weakness to cause you feel uncomfortable?
(c) Do you feel safe when you are catching our spacecraft in whole space tourism journey?
(d) If you feel unsafe, may you explain the reasons what aspects of our spacecraft has weakness to cause you feel unsafe?

Finally, we thank your ideas to be given to let us know how to improve our every time future space tourism journey in order to find what challenge cause our service performance and product quality which can not satisfy your needs. So, we shall improve to avoid future challenges continue occur. Our mission is achievement of 100% satisfactory level to our every space travelling passenger individual feeling. Also, we hope that you can choose our space tourism leisure service again, when you have another time space tourism leisure desire need. However, we shall revise to improve our service performance and product quality to be better, after collecting your ideas from this time survey investigation. I think you spend time to give your ideas from this survey investigation faithfully.

So, survey investigation method will be one important idea gathering tool to help any space tourism leisure company to revise the weaknesses to raise or improve future every time space tourism journey service performance and product quality to achieve raising competitive effort in this new space tourism leisure market.

Hence, survey investigation method will be the best idea gathering method to predict how space travelling passenger emotion or desire need will change in order to achieve the objective of raising every time space tourism journey future space travelling passenger number more easily for every space tourism leisure company.

CHAPTER THREE

How COVID disease influences global oil need and price change to impact travel leisure industry development

- The prediction of price factor influences space traveler number

The space tourism leisure organizations indicate the total cost of a trip into space is rapidly coming down from the initial price level of about US$600,000, it is obvious that the space travelling customer base is going to be rather small. Typical customers tend to belong to the top 1% income bracket. They also indicate that the price comes down , it is expected that new space travelling customer groups will enter the space tourism leisure market.

Typical new customers include people in other brackets with one-of-a kind incomes, such as inheritance or business sold. There are indications that those types of customers are becoming interested in spending on an once-in-a lifetime space experience. Therefore, the growth of the space tourism market is highly sensitive to customer satisfaction and how it is communicated through various media.

This will establish the status factors of space tourism and corresponding brand reputation service providers. They also suggest that any operator monitors space travelling customer satisfaction closely, as it will help developing increasingly accurate estimates of how the space tourism leisure market will develop.

Hence, it seems that every time space tourism journey price variable factor will influence the time space tourism of customer individual leisure desire and the space tourism passenger number. For example, the minimum price goal foe a variable space tourism business is currently estimate to be below US$3000-4000/kg for a round -trip depending on variable configuration and operation size. At this price, they estimate that somewhat over 1 % of the high income earners are potential customers.

However, for significant volume growth the longer term goal should be below US$2000/kg for a typical passenger, baggage and supplies. The lower price will probably open space tourism to a broader population, expanding the customer base and altering expectations. beyond this point space tourism will become into a travelling competitive leisure commodity, price competition will ensure and service providers need to rethink their space tourism marketing and branding and price strategies.

I shall also recommend how to attract the potential customers successfully. First, space operators need to pay special attention to the right level of customer services. Second, various preparatory customer operations cost, such as a travel to the launch site, space tourism destination accommodation, pre-flight training, medical check-ups and equipment my add up to between 10 to 15 % of the actual space travel cost. Thurs, solving the right balance between services offered and cost of client operation in order to earn the largest intangible benefits, such as loyalty, confidence, leisure enjoyment, comfortable space travelling journey as well as tangible benefits, such as profit, spacecraft manufacturing facilities, space stations, space hotels , space swimming pools, space gardens, space cinema etc. which are built to similar to earth building facilities to satisfy space travelers‘ needs.

The influential factors persuade travelers choose space tourism

Nowadays, our earth is no longer an adventurous enough place for some experienced tourists. Space tourism will be a new sector of adventure tourism, which is in the near future will be fast becoming a new tourism leisure opportunity for experiencing the unknown. Of one day, space tourism is able to reach the mass tourism phase, due to improved safety and decreased operation costs, a future space tourist will possibly only need minimal training to cope with the zero cost.

Space tourism is quite well established with visits to space attraction and launch sites, and it is a wealthy trips to the international space station for any space tourism travelers. However, if any space tourism leisure companies can attempt to find what the most influential factors are to persuade travelers feel attraction more than travelling in our earth.

It aims to let travelers to choose space travelling more than earth travelling when they feel travelling leisure need. I shall indicate what will be the most important influential factors to persuade travelers to choose space tourism more than earth tourism as below:

Firstly, I shall argue that the majority of different new space tourism journey destinations will be needed to find to satisfy different aged space travelers and different income space tourism consumers' needs. For example, the rich people have effort to consume longer time and reach any space tourism destinations where are far away from our earth of their every space tourism journey.

Otherwise, the middle income people will choose shorter space tourism journey distance from our earth and short time space tourism journey. Also, younger space tourism clients can accept more longer journey time, exciting fast speed spacecraft flying journey. Otherwise, old space tourism clients can only accept comfortable and shorter time safe space journey. So, it seems that safety, comfortable feeling, shorter time space tourism journey won't be one important influential factor to excite any young people who choose to consume space tourism leisure. Otherwise, safety, comfortable feeling, shorter time space tourism journey will be one important influential factor to excite any old people who choose to consume space tourism leisure.

Secondly, the another most important influential factor to excite space travelers to choose space tourism , it concerns whether the space travelers will feel what tourists benefits can be earned from a substantial variety of destinations choice. In general, space tourism with those of aviation, space travelers will hope space tourism will be travelling distances by air in a very short time, safely and comfortably, to bring them to arrive any space planet destinations when spacecraft reaches any space stations to stay in any space destinations.

Hence, space destination factor will bring important influential choice to any space destination journeys. As a result of the space technological tourism boom, the number of potential different space destination, choice attractions have grown with far fewer places on earth to which human do have access yet. However, the ultimate different space destinations to which many of us dream is not on earth, but as least 100 km above us, anywhere in space any planets.

If the space tourism leisure company can provide different space tourism destination choices to young or old age both space traveler target consumer groups. They will feel a real holiday when they will be able to enjoy a great image of the earth from planets. It might mean that every space tourism journey can provide different space tourism destination to let space travelers have another new travelling destinations where are far from our earth anywhere.

Hence, the different space tourism destinations will give them an unforgettable adventure. Think of how it would be to be able to check in at a " billion strategy" luxury hotel in space one planet, it means that the space planet destination can provide one luxury hotel to let space travelers to live one night or more in the space planet destination, how it would be to schedule the space traveler' vacation at one of the space tourism leisure company luxury resorts on the Moon or Mars.

This images seem from science fiction movies, but one should not forget that 100 years ago, the Wright brothers, aviation pioneers inventors and builders of the air plane, would not have imagined how, every day it is possible that future spacecraft can fly to any planets to let human have chance to stay in the space hotel one night or more.

Consequently, space destination choice and space tourism journey service performance, aviation safety, ticket price and leisure satisfactory feeling which will be important influential factors to attract future space travelers to choose space tourism leisure to replace earth tourism leisure in future one day.

● Raising space tourism leisure
consumption strategies

Although, space tourism industry is a real enjoyment and exciting travelling leisure to human. It is possible that human will choose to consume space tourism leisure to replace earth tourism leisure, if human felt that earth tourism leisure is not attractive to them to consume to go to anywhere to travel in their leisure time.

But, I believe that space tourism industry has still many factors to influence human to choose to consume space tourism leisure, even they will consider space tourism leisure consumption I is only one time space tourism in their life time. Hence, space tourism companies ought achieve this aim to persuade or attract everyone prefer to spend space tourism leisure at least one time in their life, then it can represent success. However, I think to achieve this aim, it has these challenges to influence their success, even they believe space tourism leisure business is one potential attractive travel entertainment business. These challenges include such as: expensive space tourism ticket price issue, catching spacecraft safe issue, space traveler personal body health issue, age issue, family and friend relationship influence issue, working time and holiday time arrangement issue, the space trip arrangement issue, weather issue etc. different challenges, which will have possible to influence every space tourism planner either who decide change to cancel the time space tourism plan, or forgive to choose space tourism leisure in their life forever.

Hence, how to raise space tourism leisure consumption desire will be one considerable matter for any space tourism leisure businessmen. I shall indicate my personal three aspect of strategical opinions to let them to know how to raise every space tourism planner individual space tourism leisure consumption desire to avoid every time space tourism passenger number will have decrease failure chance as below:

● (1) Strategic opinion

On the first aspect of strategic opinion, I feel that the space education tutor can teach new space knowledge to let every space traveler to learn any new space and earth knowledge during he/she is catching on the spacecraft in personal contact learning experience environment which can raise space tourism consumption desire. The reason is because the space tourism leisure traveler can raise extra space and earth learning knowledge when they can catch the spacecraft to fly and contact the space environment to learn and feel what the differences are between space and earth by himself or herself. Hence, it is very attractive to the space traveler student target group and I believe that their parents will encourage their sons or daughters to participate the time of space trip and they are more preferable to help them to buy the time space trip ticket, due to their sons and daughters can learn any space knowledge when they are studying. Moreover, every space traveler will feel surprise to learn any new space and earth knowledge from the space tutor's teaching, due to he/she is unknown that this space travel trip includes learning space and earth knowledge.

I suggest that the space tourism leisure businessmen can give learning opportunity to every travel trip space travelers to feel that this space actual environment can bring what disadvantages or advantages to influence our earth when they are catching aircraft to fly to space to travel in every space trip. The space and earth learning knowledge can include these two aspects of space learning knowledge and experience below:

On the teaching of space environment learning knowledge hand, the topics can include as below:

Firstly the space learning topic can concern how space environment influences water and hydrated minerals change , they can learn what our drinking water function how is applied to space environment. For example, in the space environment, they can learn and attempt to feel that how water can be used in protecting astronauts against harmful radiation from the sun and cosmic rays by cloaking spacecraft with a thin layer of water in the actual space environment as well as the space travelers can also feel water is same as fuel when they are catching the spacecraft, they can feel the water is heavy to transport into space when they are catching the spacecraft to fly to space during their whole space tourism journey.

Moreover, when their spacecraft reaches anyone of planets and it stays on the planet's space station, e.g. Moon space station. They can learn how to attempt to contact the hydrated minerals to learn and feel what they contained in some asteroids may be possible sources of water and fuel in the actual space environment. When they are walking in actual space environment, such as Moon planet, they can contact or touch this hydrated minerals to learn how water molecules can be extracted and separated chemically to produce hydrogen fuel knowledge in the actual space environment. This is one exciting space learning experience to the space travelling student passengers.

Secondly the space learning topic can concern how human fights space threats , even when their whole space leisure journey, the space science teacher can let the space trip student passengers to feel that they are learning new space knowledge between the space science teacher and whose space trip student passengers. Such as how to protect our earth knowledge: Teaching them to know when will be threats to our earth from space. The space science teacher can explain how this space threating environment influences our life safety and let them to feel that a mass extinction can be triggered if an asteroid 10 kilometers across hit the earth. Even being the apex species in the food chain did not space carnivorous dinosaurs from such disaster, who knows if this terrifying scene won't happen before our eyes? So, the space travelers can image and feel how the space threating environment can influence their life safety in the actual space environment as well as the space science teacher can let whose space travelers to feel and image the actual earth disaster will possible happen suddenly to let they feel afraid in the actual space environment. Also the space science teacher can teach how our earth can fright the space stones attack to let the space traveler to know, when an impactor targets an asteroid for a controlled well-times wallop. The collision will change the asteroid's momentum, deflecting it from its original orbital path which intersects with that of the earth. So, at the moment, the space travelers can image they are a larger spacecraft near an asteroid which can also change the path. Given enough time, the gravitational pull from the spacecraft will be able to steer the asteroid away from the earth. So, every space traveler will feel that they are catching the spacecraft in the safe space environment to avoid the Earth disaster from space sudden unpredictable attack.

It is more fun real space tourism knowledge learning feel to let every space traveler has chance to learn any new space science knowledge when he/she is catching the spacecraft to fly to space to travel. Hence, one successful space trip ought include trip and learning experience both contents in order to raise every the space tourism planner individual space trip consumption desire.

● (2) Strategic opinion

On the second aspect of strategic opinion, space tourism leisure companies need to let planning travelers feel that anyone of space tourism leisure is very different to general tourism leisure. In general, tourism leisure is visiting at least one night for leisure and holiday, business or other tourism purposes in Earth only. Otherwise, space tourism leisure is other kind of an unique trip leisure or entertainment method, e.g. the space traveler can catch the spacecraft to visit any planets to stay to live at the planet's space hotel at least one night, e.g. Future potential populated Moon or Mars space hotel space trip. Moreover, the space travel companies ought give chance to let them to feel what weightless feeling is in weightlessness environment when they are walking on Moon or other planets in possible. Even, they can attempt to build these entertainment facilities, instead of space hotels, such as space swimming pools, space gardens, space cinema etc. building facilities. It aims to let them to feel what the differences between Earth and space life when they are walking on the Moon, when they are swimming on the space pools, when they are living in space hotels, when they are watching movies in space cinemas, when they are seeing flowers and different species of planets and fruits. e.g. oranges, apples, bananas, and vegetable and potatoes and tomatoes in space gardens. It is very exciting and fun space trip life experience between one days to seven days. So, they believe that they must not feel these space life experience if they do not choose to participate this time space trip planning journey by the space trip company preparation.

Also, due to that the space tourism passengers need to the pre-flight checks and training before they ensure to qualify to permit to participate the space trip. So space travel companies need to concern how to take care their health check and training matter considerately. It aims to let every space traveler will feel a market segment with fitness and extreme experiences as well as he/she will become popular with a market segment passenger to the space tourism leisure company, although he/she must not guarantee to pass the space training and/or pre-flight health checks to permit to participate the space trip. However, he/she can believe that he/she is one worth space travelling passenger to the space tourism leisure company, even this time pre-flight health check or/and the short time space trip training requirements are failure. However, the space tourism leisure company must need to let all pre-flight health check and space trip training passengers to feel that it is only one space tourism which can give them and let customers view the space travel is as the ultimate showcase for health, even though a majority of the population can pass the pre-flight medical and other tests in order to raise their confidence and safety to catch the spacecraft to fly to space to travel when they are confirmed to pass these tests to permit to catch the spacecraft later.

In general, the expectations of future space passengers include the following customer value elements, such as below:

- Viewing space and the Earth.
- Experiencing weightlessness and experiencing pre-flight astronaut training and related sensations.
- Communicating from space to significant others.
- Being able to discuss the adventure in an informed way.
- Having astronaut-like documentation and memorabilia.
- Enjoying one exciting and fun space trip.

However, instead of considering these objectives need to be combined with, sometimes conflicting , constraints such as guaranteed safe, return , limited training time, reasonable comfort, and minimum medical restrictions. So, space tourism companies need to reduce every space traveler individual worries before they decide to make the time of space tourism journey. Then, it can increase their confidence to raise their space tourism consumption desire more successfully.

Consequently, instead of these consideration, a space travel operator must pay attention to the total customer experience over the entire customer process, starting from how the service is presented, proposed and sold. The service package must include training, instructions, travel to the launch site and various post. Travel activities to generate maximum customer satisfaction and brand building opportunity.

(3) Strategic opinion

On the final aspect of strategic opinion, I think any space tourism companies space tourism companies need to consider every time space tourism ticket price and space tourism trip issues. It is important factor to influence every space traveler individual consumption desire. Due to space trip ticket price must be more expensive to compare common Earth trip travelling ticket price, so this kind of tourism leisure market target customer will be the rich and high income customer group.

On the space trip ticket challenge issue, despite that fact the total cost of a trip into space is rapidly coming down from the initial price level of about US$60,000, it is obvious that the customer base is going to be rather small and the client target customer is only high income or rich consumer group. Typical customers tend to belong to the top of the top 1% income bracket. So, ensures that space traveler number must be less than common Earth traveler number.

Also, such as the space trip ticket price, it is expected that new middle rich level or middle high level income customer target group will enter the space trip leisure market, when every space trip ticket price falls down about 1% Typical new customers include people in other income brackets with one-of-a-kind incomes, such as inheritance or business sold space traveler target group. These people will be space travel new client group, when its every space trip ticket price can be reduced to close 1 to 2 % nearly. If any space tourism leisure companies expect to attract new rich and/or high income target customer group to choose any one kind of space trip journey planning to consume.

These are indications that these types of customers are becoming interested in spending on an once-in-a-lifetime space experience. Therefore, the growth of the space tourism market is highly sensitive to customer satisfaction and how it is communicated through the various media. This will establish the status –factor of space tourism, and corresponding brand reputation of service providers. The minimum price goal for a variable space tourism business is currently estimate to be below US$3-4000/kg for a round-trip depending on vehicle configuration. So, space travel leisure companies need to concern every round space trip cost, it can depend on the space vehicle number and weight issue to influence every space trip ticket price variable to achieve how much it can earn.

On space journey design factor aspect, it includes these different facilities aspects how to design, because future space travelling consumers will concern whether the space travel company can provide special entertainment to satisfy their needs. The facilities include as below:

How to design space hotels to let them to live in comfortable space environment and eat the best taste and fresh food quality when the cookers need to cook in the space hotel in the space environment? How to design space swimming pools to let them to swim in safe space environment? How to design space sport centers to let them to run more easily in one space sport warm and safe environment? How to design one space garden to let them to see different species of Earth flowers, or plants? How to design one space farming land to let them to see different species of Earth fruits, vegetables, tomatoes, potatoes etc. fresh foods growth in warm and safe space farming land environment? How to design one space cinema to let them to watch movies in one safe and warm space cinema environment? All these facilities will be any one of future space trip's' important and attractive space trip leisure facilities to influence every space traveler to choose to buy the space tourism leisure company's space trip leisure service.

Instead of these space building entertainment facilities, they also need to concern how the space vehicle entertainment tools are provided the entertainment service to satisfy their needs. When the space travelers can sit on the space vehicles to move on any planets' lands, such as Moon. A number of space vehicle options exist in the market, mainly differing based on the seat capacity as well as the in-flight experience level offered. The typical space vehicle solution is a small, relatively light weight spacecraft taking between 2 to 10 passengers. The number of passengers depends on the service level, amenities and extra offered. The trip typically lasts about 10 hours and of which about 4 hours are spent in space. The main attraction is the weightless time after in space. The main attraction is the weightless time after re-entry has started. It is a rather low-G technology and therefore the medical requirements for participants are nor very high.

Consequently, the space vehicles, space leisure building facilities, the space trip reasonable price ticket level, every safe space trip journey arrangement, clean and fresh and good taste space food arrangement, space traveler individual real learning experience etc. these factors will be the main influential factors to raise the space tourism leisure company's competitive effort and the space traveler consumer individual consumption desire to the space tourism leisure company in the future.

Space travel markting strategy

Any space travel organization needs have good marketing strategy to prepare how to operate its space travelling leisure business in order to attract many space travelling clients to choose its space travelling service. I shall indicate these different strategies aspects whey they are needed to be concerned as below:

(1) On concept of spacecraft design aspect

Firstly, on concept aspect, any one space travelling leisure company needs have at least one spacecraft to catch clients to fly to space to travel. So how to design the spacecraft and its quality and safety and comfortable environment spacecraft machine concept aspect issue which is one challenge to be concerned. Because many space travelling passengers ususally concern whether the spacecraft is safe, comfortable , good quality, as well as the space travelling leisure providers also need to concern whether the spacecraft is less time and energy saving efficient use, less manufactory operating cost and durable.

In general, space travelling leisure provider expects the spacecraft or spacecraft vehicle can be uesed long time. The spacecraft will be expected to utilize previous flight rated and proven technologies to from the basis for manufacturing spacecraft vehicles , and will incorporate the latest modern avionics and flight system for answering safety, reliability and economical operation.

In general, the spacecraft will be designed to carry two crew and approximately, 10,000 pounds of cargo, depending on the ultimate weight of the spacecraft. Relying on flight hardware to maintain the space station, such as Moon or Mar space station is fpr any space travelling spacecrafts to reach these space travelling destinations to stay, it is also need to consider by many space travelling experts as risky, extremely, expensive cost sensitive for any space station travelling destination design arrangement in order to future every spacecraft can fly to any planets to stay on its space station safely.

● Outsourcing spacecraft concept design strategy

As a result, outsourcing strategy is one good method to help them to reduce cost in order to achieve to let every space travel passenger has safe space journey experience and capacity for safely launching a fully loaded (including crew and cargo). Outsourcing strategy is the launch role to a major contracor, they can concentrate on crew flight training, planning all passnegers and cargo capacoty, and preparing flight manifests, and will as a result, avoid the expense of maintaining a launch operation on a daily basis. In addition, by outsoucing the spacecraft manufacturing, the space travelling provider can avoid spending millions of dollars on facilities and equipment infrastructure and engineering manufacturing expertise.

(2) On deciding misson aspect

Secondly, on mission aspect, any space travelling journey needs have a clear mission to be planned how to achieve in order to ensure every space travelling passenger feel satisfactory in the space travelling journey. So, every whole space travelling journey arrangement, e.g. where will be the space travelling destination, how to check every space travelling planned passengers' bodies whether who are health to catch spacecraft to fly to space to travel or how to train every space travelling planned passenger to ensure whom can permit to catch spacecraft to fly to space to travel, how to arrange every space travelling journey entertainment and facilities to let either young or old age target passenger to enjoy the space trip to feel satisfactory, how to arrange different days of every space trip.

In the last few years, Virgin Galactic has been making new's headlines with its promises to provide space travel services, and announcement that it will soom offer, at quite a hefty price, trips to sub-orbit. It is generally agreed that sub-orbit exists 100 kilometres above the earth's sea-level (Von Der Dunk, 2012). Hence, Virgin Galactic will provide travel to where customers may experience weightlessness, as well as the sight of earth's curvature. Even more interesting is that Virgin Galactic is not the only company with such a mission,there are a few more that wish to offer the same type of service. For example, some companies even aim to provide an orbital type of flight.

Orbit flight suggests that humans would venture into outer space, where they might either orbit the earth or board the international space station (hereinafter: ISS). In addition, some envision space hotels, moon visitations and mining asteroids. Although at first such statement might seem for one must point out that a "space hotel" is already in earth's orbit and that diligent progress through flight tests is almost made the commercial aspect of regular space travel a reality; it is only the question of time and readiness for the companies to make their long-awaited and open a new industry of present day economics (Klemm & Markkanen, 2011; Berry , 2012).

So, every space travelling mission is to ensure that reliable, technologically-sophisicated competitively-priced flight certified spacecraft are designed and properly maintained when performing their every assigned space travelling journey mission. The space traveller leisure provider will need to provide a carefully selected array of techologies that are capable of meeting the requirements of travelling into earth orbit. It will emphasize affordability, reliability, safety, customer service and responsiveness in responding to customer's space travelling requirements.

For this space tourism leisure mission example, it many include these objectives , such as below:

One trip into space, sending a space vehicle of a certain make and with a specify capacity on a space mission, provides the various grades of a core service, such as a space mission including issues such as waiting and delivery times, personal attention and advice, amenities and facilities, ensure quality assurance, it is the planned and system activities implemented in a quality system. So that quality requirements for a product or service will be fulfilled. It aims at preventing high-risk adverse events, or reducing thei impact, provides excellent customer satisfaction, it is a measure of how products and services meet the space travelling customer expectations, customer satisfaction is also always evaluated in relationship of every space travelling ticket price of the space travelling entertainment service and spacecraft product comfortable environment feeling and good leisure arrangement for every space travelling leisure journey.

(3) On space tourism leisure organization managment aspect

Thirdly, on space tourism leisure organization management aspect, it is also important to influence efficient and excellent space service performance to be provided to satisfy every space travel organization management team needs to be consists of experienced professionals who have successfully management and operated companies specializing in the aerospace industry for a number of years.

Their knowledge and contacts within the space industry will prove invaluable in assisting the space tourism leisure provider in the achievement of its goals and objectives. In individuals on the team components that up a spacecraft tourism development organization, and have unique experience in the design, construction, operations and maintenance of the major functions will developing spacecraft for launching into orbit. Every spacecraft will be built and maintained utilizing the same high standards of quality, within budget and well within time constraints.

Hence, every space tourism provider needs have one excellent management leaders to manage every space tourism service staffs to serve passengers in order to achieve excellent service performance to let them every one to feel satisfactory, during their every space tourism journey (trip).

(4) On target audience prediction aspect

On target audience prediction aspect, every space trip needs have identifies target travelling passenger in order to concentrate to choose the most popular and satisfactory space travelling journey for their identified needs.

For primary audiences example, it can include space enthusiasts and educational families both. Space enthusiasts target are usually young people and they are only 20% over 65 age old people target space ethusiasts who will be the future potential space tourism target consumers as well as the educational families target who will aspect owning educational experience for children , who is the explicit reason to visit space, either he/she has interest in history of space exploration or he/she has interest in future of space exploration or he/she feels that spce trip looked like fun.

KSCVC Visots (2013) indicated that future top markets, ranked by high visitation against space enthusiasts and educational families space tourism passengers, the US cities will include: Orlando, NYC, Miami, Tampa Bay, Chicago, West plam, Philadelphia, Atlanta, Boston, Washington, DC and San Francisco cities. So, future US space travelling market will be the top one in the world.

(5) On space objective aspect

On space objective aspect, instead of any one space tourism leisure organization concerns how to achieve its mission to satisfy all space tourism passengers leisure needs. Although, it is the major missin for space tourism leisure industry. But they can not neglect what the objectives are in order to develop or achieve long term space tourism leisure missions more easily.

The objectives main open space key issues can include such as: Providing an adequate supply of land to meet the future needs of strategic opn space links, natural areas and recreational facilities on any future space tourism destinations, increasing pressure for public access to open space areas with conservation values, competing interests between adjoining land use and development on public open space and its user groups, use of public open space and recreational resources for drainage purposes, raising higher space traveller hotel residential development placing increased pressure on the demand for public open space planet land use aim and developing public open space mor intensive leisure and sport activities on any future new space tourism planet destinations.

When the space tourism leisure providers have long term objectives to attempt to solve above these any one of key issues. It will ahve a more clear objective to achieve its long term space tourism leisure business market. It's long term objectives can include such as below:

To identify existing and future active and passive recreation needs and social trends of future space tourism visitors; to provide a wide range of high quality and accessible public open space public land areas to encourage physical activity and social interaction to meet the existing and future needs of space travelling visitors; to identify existing gaps in the public open space network and develop any different kinds of space trip arrangement to satisfy the different identified target space traveller individual needs; to protect enhance and increase landcrapt values of public open space land use; to recognize the hierarchy of public open space assets; equitably distributing open space resources; access to facilities and a diverse range of opportunities to incorporate the drainage function in public open space travelling destination areas without detriment to safely, environmental, visual and recreational values.

So, these development of any space planets howo to use their lands objectives will bring long term space travelling destination beneficial advantages to raise to build the space hotels, space swimming pools, space gardens, space cinemas, space sport places to let future space travelers can stay in Mars or Moon planet destinations to enjoy these leisure facilities and they can feel which are similar to our earth leisure facilities attractively.

These space buildings are important to attract future space travellers to catch spacecraft to fly to Mars or Moon planet to travel in possible because it is fun and exciting space trip when these leisure facilities can be built on Moon or Mars to let space travellers to stay short days in either these two planets to live their space hotels. So how to build any one of these space leisure building which is another important objective for any future space tourism leisure business, instead of how to arrange any space destination trip objective. So, any space tourism leisure provider ought not neglect how to achieve these two main space tourism objectives.

However, these are key questions continually asked regarding the viability of space tourism. They concern financial, marketing and political communities. Their concerns can be best addredded in a properly, comprehensive business plan. Some questions can not be answered definitively at this time. Hoever, knowledge of the concerns and developing space businesses in any space traveling leisure planning stages and efforts to raise capital in the following questions, every spce tourism leisure business leader needs to concern this questions as below:

Can the space tourism industry into a profitable enonomic industry?

Are challenges related to financing, marketing, business methodologies or a combination of all of these facets?

Can the proponents of space tourism to be proven business tools and methodologies in their presentation of an acceptable business plan?

Can at least a cost effective, certified passenger space tourism journey to be developed for space tourism?

What effects will influence space-tourism businesses of NASA begins selling seats on the US space shuttle to civilian space tourists?

All above questions will be every new space tourism leisure businessman who needs to concern questions in order to achieve whose marketing strategy more successfully. Consequently, marketing strategy is important to be prepared in order to follow corrective steps to achieve every space tourism leisure business missions and objectives more easily.

● Space tourism leisure behavioral economic consumption model

In space tourism leisure industry, due to every time space trip needs the space travelling planner to plan how much budget to consume expensive spce ticket price. So, it seems that the target customers will be rich or high income level young people or the retirement rich old people target customer group.

So, it brings this question: How to persuade these rich or high income young people or rich retirement old people to prefer to spend spce tourism leisure at least one time in their life?

It is one valuabe research question to every future space tourism leisure provider. I shall indicate the successful factors to analyze how to persuade them to accept this kind of potential space travelling leisure in behavioral economic personal consumption view point, in order to explain the cause and effect relationship between of these factors as below:

(1) Economic environment variable factor

Firstly, it is economic environment variable factor whether it can influence to space tourism leisure consumption changing. As I discuss about economic environment variable issue will influence consumption behavior changing. For space tourism leisure case, it is not now kind of essential consumption leisure product to every one. So , even the rich or high income people who will be influences to seek this kind of leisure to play, it the economic environment is improved, it will influence they have positive attitude and interest to choose this kind of leisure consumption. However, if the economic environment is worse, it will influence they have negative attitude and no interest to choose this kind of leisure consumption, due to space travel is one kind of expensive leisure consumption to every one.

Hence, in this space tourism leisure industry, it does not ensure that the rich or high income people must be persuade to choose this kind of expensive space tourism entertainment in whose holiday or retirement time. They can have the common tourism entertainment to go to different countries to travel many times in our earth. Otherwise, space tourism leisure is more expensive to compare common earth tourism leisure , it means that the rich or high income people only spend one time spacecraft catching to fly to space to travel in their life, it is more difficult to every space traveler like to catch spacecraft to fly to space to travel more than one time, due to he/she had attempted to catch spacecraft to fly to space to travel to own space travel experience, he/she will feel enough satisfactory and enjoyment in common. Hence, it is possible that future many rich or high income people only like to spend one time space tourism leisure, then they won't continue to spend this kind of tourism entertainment again in their life.

Thus, space tourism leisure providers need to arrange any special or attractive space tourism leisure to persuade these high income or rich target clients to consume, when the economic environment will change worse. The Europen space agency (ESA), defines this phenomenon between economic environment variable and space tourism client growth or falling number relationship as: " space tourism is an execution of sub-orbital flight by privately finded and/or privately operated vehicles and the technology development driven by space tourism market."

it seems that space vehicle is one attractive travelling desire tool will be one attractive selling point to influence space tourism leisure consumer individual entertainment choice or attitude to be changed to positive leisure consumption attitude to prefer to play this kind of space tourism activities when economic environment changes to worse. Hence, when economic environment is worse, the economic wore changing factor will influence the space travelling planner individual leisure consumption desire, even it will influence the rich or high income young people or rich retirement people target customer both groups.

As (ESA, 2008) indicated space vehicle will be one kind of attractive leisure tool for spce traveler. So, I suggest that space tourism lesiure journey arrangement needs to include that such as : the space travelers can catch space vehicle to move on Moon or Mars plants land to feel what the different feeling is between during they are catching public transportation tool, such as bus or taxi during the are catching these transportation tools on earth land and during they are catching space vehicle tools on Mars or Moon planet's lands. It is so exicting and fun catching space vehicle tool experience on these both Mars or Moon planets' lands to the young and old age space travelling passengers. Because every space vehicle's speed is not very fast and it will move on Moon or Mars planets slowly. So, any aged pace travelling passengers can attempt to play this kind of space facilities leisure after they catched spacecraft to fly to these both Mars or Moon planet to stay. They can spend half hour or one hour, even more than one hour to catch the space vehicle to go to anywhere on Mars or Moon to travel. It is possible that they can find exciting and undiscovered things on these both planets.

So, catching space vehicle to go to anywhere on either these both planets journey, it will one essential part of space travelling journey during the economic environment is changed to worse. It is extra attractive space travelling leisure journey to attract space tourism consumer individual leisure desire when economic environment is worse.

Hence, from this perspective then space tourism could be understood as a section of the tourism industry mainly based on technological development, progression and its activitity being related specifically to sub orbital flights. So, if future space tourism providers expect whether the global economic environment changing will be better or worse which won't influence space tourism leisure consumption desire to be changed. The space tourism leisure providers need to persuade the space tourism planners feel space tourism would have to be treated like an already exciting part of the tourism industry. It means that space tourism leisure is one kind of tourism leisure choice to replace common earth tourism leisure consumption. When travelers feel space tourism is another tourism leisure to replace which can replace common earth tourism leisure. It will avoid the worse economic environment changing factor to reduce the rich or high income young people or rich retirement old people whose space travelling leisure consumption desire.

Consequently , the question in relation to, in what kinds of space tourism journey message do space travel providers promote behind whether space vehicle journey promotion message which is needed when economic environment will change worse. I shall be asked, as understanding the meaning in which space tourism is being marketed, communicated is seen as a factor , which can either positively contribute to future development of the tourism industry or lead into prolonging or seen stopping the space tourism industry from its progression.

(2) Space tourism leisure journey management factor

Secondly, space tourism leisure jounrey management factor, how to arrange every space tourism leisure journey which will be one important factor to influence space tourism planner individual tourism consumption desire.

In general, it can includes these several forms of space tourism leisure activities in every space lesiure trip arrangement. The following classification of space tourism include: Terrestria spce tourism (i.e. NASA visit centre, space movies, online space experience); Atmospheric space tourism (i.e. : MIG 31 flight, zero G. flights) and astro (orbita) tourism (i.e.: trips to the international space station-beyond earth orbit) (Cater 2010, Crouch et al. 2009).

Instead of US domestic space tourism market is potential, next country is Japan. First, the study is made by Collins et. al (1994, 1996) in Japan on 3030 research participants, showed that 80% of respondents under the age of 50 were willing to travel to space and out of them 20% were willing to pay year's salary for the space travel experience. Yet, it could be citicized that the Japan people age group of under 50 could be too broad, in general different generations under one groups. nest besides the willingness to go to space, the Japanese study showed respondents motivations for travelling to space, including any fun and exciting attractive space tourism journey, e.g. interest in space walk, catching space vehicle or driving space vehicle on the either Moon or Mars planets, earth view, zeo gravity experience, livin gin space hotels one night or more, watching movies in space cinemas, swimming in space pools, visiting space gardens, running in space sport centers, catching spacecrafts to view earth or Moon or Mars planets.

Hence, it seems attractive space tourism journey can persuade another country's space travelling planners, such as Japanese attempts to satisfy whose space tourism needs. So, different kinds of attractive space trip journey arrangement will be one important factor to influence young and old age travelling consumption desire. It implies that attractive space tourism journey will be one influential factor to encourage other countries tourism consumers attempt to another kind of leaving earth tourism leisure. So, any space tourism trip destinations and leisure facilities arrangement must need to satisfy space traveler individual leisure needs and every space trip must be more fun, exciting and comfortable and enjoyable feeling to compare general tourism journey in earth. Due to general earth tourism leisure will be space tourism leisure's competitive or replaced leisure product and service. Hence, space trip destinations and leisure facilities choice will be one important factor to influence space travelling planner's consumption desire.

Every space travelling planner will compare general earth travelling leisure's destinations and leisure facilities arrangement whether the space travelling trip arrangement , leisure facilities arrangement and food arrangement, space vehicle or spacecraf leisure comfortable influence issues which will have more satisfactory enjoyable feeling to compare general earth tourism leisure and their spending expenditure to every space trip whether is value or is not value.

Consequently, economic environment changing factor and space trip and leisure facilities arrangement factor which both will influence any space tourism planner individual consumption desire mainly. So, space tourism businessmen ought concern these two aspects of factors how and when will change to adapt any country's potential space traveler's space tourism changing taste and needs in order to follow the new space tourism changing needs easily.

Space tourism market moral ethic risk threats

What are space tourism moral ethic risk during the space businessmen operate this businesses as well as what market threats who will encounter to face difficulties ? I shall give actul cases to explain how and why these challenges will cause to influence any new space tourism businesses development successfully.

(1) Potential accidents aspect

Firstly, space travelers will concern that public reactions to potential accidents aspect during they are catching spacecrafts to travel to space. In fact, it is moral ethic responsibility to any space tourism leisure providers to provide safe, comfortable and non accident occurrence in their whole space trip. Because once time accident will cause any one of space passenger hurt or death. So , it must be any space tourism businessmen responsibilities to concern whether they have enough confidence to ensure none any accident occurrences in every space tourism trip.

Hence, in space tourism industry, government needs have public policy to threaten or prohibit any space tourism leisure providers neglect to often check and ensure any spacecraft machines or equipments are regular opeations, as well as often renew new spacecraft machines when they are old to be used. The policy is a force effort to need them to abide every space tourism leisure safe responsibility to ensure or guarantee any one of spacecraft won't have accident occurrences during it has left earth to fly to space in whole space trip journey from the beginning to the end till to the spacecraft come to earth safely.

Hence, this policy forces any space tourism leisure providers concern to put a monetary value on increased or reduced risk of death, the " value of statistical live", used to characterize when the benefit of safety regulation is worth the cost such regulation improves. So, the country government and the country's space tourism leisure providers both have responsibilities to guarantee all space tourism passengers' life safety. It must not allow any death or hurt occurrences during every space tourism trip.

Even, the country government can have legal action to publish any space tourism leisure providers, when their every space tourism trip has occurred accidents, e.g. fire accident occurrence in spacecarft or spacecrat machines are broken to be damaged and need to be repaired during the space tourism trip. It will threaten to reduce trip accident occurrence, such as this cases. The commercial space ventures may present risk to property as well, such as a fire starting on the ground by launch-related material or problems presented by space debris.

In principle, liability law can provide incentive to deter carelessness that could lead to the destruction of property, although statutory (rather than common law) assignments of liability for commercial launches are somewhat problematic.

Consequently, if the space tourism leisure provider expected to grow space tourism passenger number in long -term time, it must need to ensure none any accidents can occur during any space trip. Otherwise, the space tourism passengers can choose another space tourism leisure provider to replace its spce tourism leisure easily.

(2) Space tourism destinations and space tourism entertainment facilities safe arrangement challenges aspect

Secondly, it is space tourism destinations and space tourism entertainment facilities safe arrangement challenges. Nowadays, commercial space travel is looking more like a real possibility than science fiction. The usual ethical issues related to the safety of the space destination choices and the space tourism entertainment facilities, e.g. space vehicles, space hotels, space swimming pools, space sport centers, space cinemas, space gardens, space farming lands. In this strange space environment and safety concerns are just the beginning as there are othe interesting questions, such as below:

What likely would be a fair process for commercializing or claiming property in any space planets? Such as Moon or mars, when any future space tourism leisure providers who need to build above these any one of space entertainment facilities on these planets to provide to their space travelling customers to play.

How to distribute and manage these any lands ownership to these future space tourism providers fairly and legally?

How likely would a separatist movement be among space settlements to want to be free and independent states?

How to ensure above future space entertainment facilities and space entertainment places are in the safe space environment to be provided to any space travelers to play in any planets, e.g. Moon or Mars etc. planets.

So, concerning how to arrange space entertainment facilities to provide to space tourism clients to play in any safe space environment issue, it will be another concerning question to every space tourism leisure providers. When they decide to choose anywhere to the space hotels, space swimming pools, space gardens, space cinemas or space farming lands or space sport centers. These space buildings will need to be built in the safe, on stable stone lands environment and none any natural distaster, such as large wind or space underground water etc. unpredictable space natural distasterr attack to these space buildings suddenly. Because it has responsibility to any space tourism leisure providers to guarantee any one of these space buildings are safe to be built in the planet's safe land environment. It aims to achieve none any accident occurrences during their space tourism clients are staying to enter these any one of space buildings to visit or play any space entertainment facilities safely, e.g. space vehicle.

So, they must need to ceck anywhere the space planet's places to be ensured safe to build any buildings. Then, they can choose the suitable locations to build space entertainment facilities or buildings more confidently.

In fact, any space entertainment facilities, e.g. space hotels, space farming lands as well as space transportation tools, e.g. spce vehicle, spacecraft , these things will be value to be concerned to any space tourism leisure providers and it is business moral ethic responsibility to every one of them, when they plan to develop their space tourism business in any planets.

(3) Space tourism market competition challenge aspect

Thirdly, any provate space tourism development leisure businesses will face market competitive challenge, such as large spacefaring countries, e.g. US, UK have possible to dominate future space tourism leisure business (government can own space tourism leisure business). They will be main actors in space were nation-states. Large spacefaring counties can build the space vehicles, that can take people and cargo into orbit and to the Moon, or Mars crafted international space law and shaped the main investments in space tourism leisure technology.

So, it is possible that the own space technological developed countries, such as US, UK, these countries governemts will have possible to operate public fund to support space tourism leisure business. It implies that private space tourism leisure businesses will face public space tourism leisure business and themselve private space tourism leisure business market competition in space tourism leisure industry.

If these two countries governments also participate this private space tourism leisure market. It will raise market threats to any private space tourism organizations.

Whether will developed countries governments participate private space tourism market? It is possible that new commercial actors began to enter the space tourism leisure industry, looking to disrupt both space launch services ans use space in new exotic ways. For example, the US government also moved its purposeful degradatoin of the global positioning system (GPS), so US government will have effort to dominate GPS global positioning system communication business also. As this GPS communication business case, future US government has possible to decide to participate space tourism leisure business also.

However, in the future, space tourism leisure industry may contribute even more the developed countries, e.g. American, England economy. Space tourism and resource recovery, e.g. mining on planet, Moons and asteroids in particular may become large parts of that space tourism industry if these countries governments participated to this space tourism industry development. Of course, their viability rests on a range of factors, including costs , future regulation, international market competivitive problems and assumption about space technological development. However, these is increasing optimism in these areas of economic production to bring human space tourism leisure enjoyment and space mining resource development benefits. But the space economy is not just about what happens in orbits or how that alters life on the ground. The growth of this economy can also contribite to new innovations across all future possible unpredictable or undiscovered technological development, instead of space tourism leisure or space mining resource exploitation development.

Consequently, any space development technological governments will have possible to bring economic benefits from either only private space tourism leisure organizations or governments and private space tourism leisure both organizations cooperate to participate to achieve space tourism misson to contribute to global economic development and create new jobs to be employed in space labor supply market.

● Can space tourism business bring
economy benefits

It is fact that space tourism activities have a positive and beneficial impact on eveyday life and society and this help space travelers to understand that, despite the high space ticket prices of any space tourism leisure choices. However, space tourism will bring scientific knowledge and technological knowhow and jobs to bring humn tangible or untangible both benefits. I shall indicate these benefits as below:

Although, space tourism leisure seems only leisure activities to be consumed to satisfy any space tourism individual travelling need. However, it can assign space scientists to research and attempt discovery these intangible benefits: Such as tele-communications revolution, satellite weather forecasting, mapping mineral exploration, water resource management diaster mitigation, national security or other undiscovered untangible benefits. Because every spacecraft needs to plan to fly to space, and it will reach any space planet stations, e.g. Mars, Moon planet when it visits these any one planet, the space scientists can attempt to find new undiscovered space resource , e.g. mining or finding new undiscovered satellite weather forecasting method when they can reach these planets to attempt to do space scientifical investigtion to research new space resource , or find any space stones attack to our methods to avoid earth disaster occurrence (national security mission), instead of the spacecraft catchs space passengers to visit these planets to enjoy these planets space entertainment facilities in their space trip journeys.

(1) On space resource benefit aspect

Hence, the space tourism intangible benefits include: space exploration and international cooperation is developing sophisticted space technologies by nations. For example, the images of distant stars and glaxies using Hubble telescope, research laboratory such as international space station to conduct experiments in biology, human biology, physics, Astronomy and meteorology under microgravity environment and testing of the spacecraft systems will be required for space tourism missions to the Moon and Mars. In the future, human would be able to have unlimited and clean solar energy from space for our industries as well as heating and lighting our homes. In the near future , it would be possible to disposed-off our nuclear waste safely and unexpensively and released towards the sun using a space elevator. We many become a space tourist in earth orbit or on the Moon or Mars. We may carry and extra-terrestial mining and even introduce the development of a multi-planet economy.

(2) On education benefit aspect

Another on education benefit aspect, space tourism can let space travelers to feel actual space learning experiences, during the spacecraft is flying in the space. Their space environment learning experience can include, for example: How many spacecraft have been launched by a given country? How many phone calls are made over a satellite? How many lives could be saved by resue satellites? How they feel differences when they are living in one space hotels, they are swimming in the swimming pools, they are visiting the space garden, they are running in one space sport centers, they are visiting in one space farming land, they are sitting or driving one space vehicle on planet land, or they are catching one spacecraft.

These space learning experience will let they feel what the actual differences between space environment and earth environment. It is one humankind learning experience education service in any space planet's Moon or Mars remote areas, bringing information and tourism entertainment facilities to the masses. The space experience learning knowledge can provide data to let these space travelers to know, such as how ships can be safe at sea, monitoring the threat of pollution, how enhancing durable medical instruments for better health-care enabling hikers and skiers to be located when lost, many more. So, it seems space tourism can bring much positive benefits as no negative impact on space activitied has been found by the society , the investments are made by the nations on space activites are justified and not the waste of money.

● What are the tangible social and economic benefits brought from space tourism?

In most advanced economies space tourism or space resource exploitation industry is seen as an enabler that improves lives and helps to develop both economic and social spheres. Space industry economic can include these aspect: Application of space technology to space tourism navigation, meteorological forcasting and broadcast of on live television and internet connectivity to lesser-known applications, such as precision agriculture, transport, tracking, resource extraction and monitoring of utility networks.

Additional application exists in the disaster monitoring and relif, insurance and military applications. Thus, data coming from satellites is important to all economic sectors, making the world a better and safer place.

International space tourism experience would suggest that space travelling leisure businesses deliver value by providing a central point for academia industry , defence and foreign entities to collaborate among themselves and with government and to facilitate the flow of knowledge and capital.

How can space tourism industry maximize the socio-economic benefits? In fact, our growing use of space derived data and systems is our growing dependence on a better and safer sapce planet, e.g. Moon or Mars and to provide space tourism safe services that space travelling service that space traveler all benefit from industry in telecommunication , health, transport , banking , security and climate change monitoring.

The space tourism positive influence result is long term, the positive contribution to our quality of life is real. In other word, the world for space tourism leisure activities is changing the internationally space tourism

sector is experiencing a profound revolution.
In conclusion, space tourism leisure countries with historical leadership in space tourism have been under positive as a result of a tough financial environment leading to the definition of their space travelling technology priorities. In the meantime, new space entertainment travelling leaders, such as US, UK , even China, India have ambitions in space tourism through massive investments in the development of their capabilities in space travelling leisure business aspect.
So, the future space travelling entertainment market is large, due to China and India both have many rich people and high income people, who expect to consume in space tourism leisure trip at least one time in their lifes. Consequently, worldwide space tourism entertainment industry players are rethinking their busines models and strategies as they experience discuptive innovations, competitive space tourism entertainment and new drivers impacting the spacecraft and any space entertainment facilities manufacturing on Moon or Mars planet, launch and space tourism entertainment related businesses. Thus, we can in fact in talk about a new space tourism business, in which more and more innovative applications of space tourism data are developed dependence on space tourism data in everyday life rises and increasing share of economic growth relies on the space tourism market both in terms of opportunity benefits , e.g. India and China spce tourism potential market development and any concern space tourism job creation to every countries. Hence, space tourism development can bring positive economic benefits to any countries.

Space flight safe factor

To operate one space flight exploration organization, it needs to concern human safe flight factor. I shall indicate it needs to have these three stages to further develop its space exploration to continue to improve its safe space flight for every time of space flight.
Human future space flight missions will include these three stages to continue journey into space. The first stage is short term, NASA's return to flight after the Columbia accident. The second stage is mid term. What is needed to continue flying the shuttle fleet until a replacement means for human access to space and for other shuttle capabilities is available, and the third stage is long term, future directions for the kinds in space. Therefore, the space exploration organization can arrange the three stages to carry out any future space exploration activities. I believe it can improve every time

of space flight more safe because it can ensure its space rocket engineering can be improved to raise safe level to let space people to catch to leave our Earth.

However, any human future space flight, which must be enhanced safety of flight when carry on any experimenting space flight exploration missions. Because NASA's safety performance is a very important factor to influence any space people confidence to catch every sky rocket to leave our Earth to do any space exploration activities. So, eliminating and catching rocket risks will be any beginning and end than during the middle of any space flight exploration journeys.

Space people's life is the most important assets of any space exploration journeys. Because of the dangers of ascent and re-entry, because of unknown space environment and because we are still relative new comers, operation of shuttle and indeed all human space flight must be viewed as a development activity.

Thus, any every time space flight exploration missions will need to encourage to invent new space transportation engines (machine) or fuel, e.g. nuclear fuel to reduce the any space exploration journey accident risks and achieves to spend the fastest time to arrive any new space exploration destination. Thus, I believe any new space exploration flight will improve the space transportation technology and invent more new fuel and new space rocket manufacturing materials for future human any unknown space exploration flight demand. The three stages of improving space transportation include as below:

The beginning stage, for example, the space shuttle is as somehow comparable to civil or military air transport. They are not comparable; the inherent risks of spaceflight are serious higher. The recognition of human spaceflight as a developmental activity requires a shift in focus from operations and meeting schedules to a concern for the risks involves. Thus, the space transportation tools will be improved to protect space passengers safety: the improving the ability to tolerate it, repairing the damage on a timely basis, reducing unforeseen events from the loss of crew and vehicle, exploring all options for survival, such as provisions for crew escape systems and safe havens , barring unwarranted departures from design standards and adjusting standards only under the most safety-driven process.

The mid-term stage, the present shuttle is not very safe to fly in space. Thus, focus on safe return to flight is very important to every space flight journey rules , they leave Earth and arrive any another new planet destination, then come back our Earth again in every space exploration journey (flight). Thus, the energy will be space transportation tool one important factor. If the space transportation tool has enough supply, which won't stay in space and can not fly in space suddenly. Thus, the every time of the human space flight will be taken more time and effort then would be reasonable to expect prior to return to flight. Thus, human space exploration organization needs have higher reliability organization structure to manage every space flight, e.g. one is separating technical authority from the function of managing schedules and cost. Another is an independent safety and mission assurance organization.

It is the capability for effective systems integration perhaps even more challenging than these organizational changes are the cultural changes requires. Thus, the cultural to safe and effective space rocket operations are real and substantial. If the space exploration organization has good culture to let every staffs can communicate easily. I believe the every time space exploration accident will be reduced. Examples include: the tendency to keep knowledge of problems contained within a center or program, technical decisions, without in -depth, peer-reviewed technical analysis, and an unofficial hierarchy or system created by placing excessive power in one office. Such factors interfere with open communication, the shared of lesson learned, cause duplication and expenditure of resources and create a burden for managers to reduce undesirable characteristics threaten safety.

Thus, any space exploration trip, rocket equipment safety and check are very important factor to prepare for every time space flight. The reason is that space flight must guarantee any space people who can come back Earth, if the rocket equipment are poor and lack maintenance. The, the space people whose life is dangerous. Due any space exploration organization mission require human presence in space. For example, president John Kennedy's 1961 charge to send Americans to the moon and return then safely to Earth. Thus, the space exploration organization has attempted to carry out a similar high priority mission that would justify the expenditure of resources on a scale equivalent to those allocated for project Apollo. Also, the space exploration organization has had to participate in the give and take of the normal political process in order to obtain the resources needed to carry out its programs.

Another main successful factor in the final stage, the space exploration organization needs have a clearly defined long term space mission to commit over the past decade to improve future space exploration flight safety by developing a second generation space transportation system. So, for long term, the space exploration organization should need to plan for future space transportation capabilities without making them dependent on technological breakthroughs.

For example, mission for a post Apollo effort that involved full development of low-Earth orbit, permanent outposts on the moon, and initial journeys to Mars planet. Since that rejection, these objective, have reappeared as central elements in many proposals, setting a long term vision for any space exploration flight programs in the future.

Thus, space organization future space exploration mission for 21 St century is to lead the exploration and development of the space frontier, advance science, technology and enterprise and building institutions and systems that make accessible vast new resources and support human settlements beyond Earth orbit from the highland of the Moon to the plains of Mars. Thus, the space exploration organization limit is to conduct the research required to plan missions to Mars and/or other distant destinations. This is the most safe space flight distance limit by the space rocket equipment, machine installation , quality and effort to guarantee space people life safety when who catch the space rocket life safety when who catch the rocket to leave Earth to arrive any space destination in any space flight. However, human travel to destinations beyond Earth orbit has not been adopted because it is too far space flight to cause accident risk. Hence, space exploration organization future invention of long term need is that the role of new space transportation capabilities in enabling whatever space goals need to choose to pursue for human present in Earth orbit vision.

In conclusion, space exploration organization needs to in-depth examination space shuttle safe issue, how to reach an inescapable design of the space shuttle, because that the design was based in many aspects on how absolute technologies and because the space shutter is now an aging system , but still developmental in character, it is in the space organization is interest to replace the shuttle as soon as possible as the primary aim for transporting humans to and from Earth orbit.

- Space exploration organization mission and strategy

Space exploration organization communication strategy

I recommend any space exploration organization needs to the message concerns how the role of humans are actual physical presence in space exploration missions succeed. Because the positive message will give good idea of space exploration and then design and build means to carry out right space exploration direction to let humans to know whether any space exploration missions‘ goals, objectives and what humans benefits (welfares) who can earn.

The message includes such as these primary role of humans, therefore, is to provide the inspiration and create the vision which produces the motivation in those who then go on to make it a reality, e.g. the space exploration mission is to bring their human intellectual capability to bear in designing the technical systems required for space transportation and devising the scientific experiments associated with space exploration from its beginnings.

Thus, any space exploration organization needs to let humans to know whether what benefits humans will earn after it carries out any space exploration experiments possibly. I believe that the exploration of the Earth's great expanse (the sea, the undersea world, air and land) is the ultimate role played by humans in body and in mind, and apply their intelligence, emotions and most importantly of all, their superior cognitive performance. So, this is the role now played by astronauts, explorers in the true sense of the world.

Why does space exploration organization need to be the role of communicator? The reason is because there is the role that space organization's need to play as communicators, journalists or other communication professional. It is they who provide the link between those involved in the project and taxpayer, who are entitled to be informed about the fascinating news on space.

Moreover, space exploration organization staffs need to give message to let humans to know why these playing roles are entirely human specific and can not be fulfilled by machines. For example, roles prior to human intervention, such as accompanying humans and performing tasks, which are repetitive and unpleasant out satellites too high a risk. By sending out satellites to explore our solar system humans have already begun to explore universe into reality Robots. On the other hand, may be things, but they are not visionaries and nor are they inventors or explorers. Any achievement they accomplish are in fact space organization staffs who designed and programmed them. Also, humans remain the best available cognitive machine in any environment that may be subject to significant variations relative to the model initially made of it. Thus, space exploration organization needs to explain, such as why in the general context of space exploration, even of most missions are robotic, remains technology challenges, it presents push engineers to the very limits of what can be achieved.

In the future, humans will earn these benefits or from any space explorations new invention possibly, such as fuel cells, the microcomputer, high performance materials, medical advances, new management techniques for major projects, quality and reliability control in industry etc. The most important space exploration organization needs to positive message to let these groups of people to human what which is doing in our societies. Then, which will cause different actors to become involved from thinkers, visionaries and inspirational figures in the form of writers and film makers to scientists, engineers, philosophers, politicians, economists, physicians, journalists, authors, space travelers (astronauts), but also adults and children space story book readers alike. Thus, space exploration organization is truly multi disciplinary enterprise. Moreover, in the present day, normal escapes being concerned by space, as much due to its contribution to daily life and the knowledge it beings of the Solar system and the universe. It seems space exploration organization will influence human past history will be changed to develop. Whether it brings positive or negative change. The space organization must have responsibility to keep its any space exploration missions leader position in our Earth. It implies it is also one social responsible organization for future global human benefit (welfare).

Also space exploration organization needs to let humans know what it's future aims (intentions) are to let humans know whether why it plan to implement. Such as it needs to choose destination has typically been the Moon, it had increasingly come to focus its attention on Mars and even further afraid. Moreover, it also needs to know humans to know the modes of future space transportation which described have tended to be those of the period concerned: ships, horses, birds, balloons, canons, rockets and even others of a more esoteric nature, even solar sail or nuclear soil further space transportation technology development. In addition, space exploration organization can need to describe where are further orbital space stations in space different locations and explained the various applications of satellites and spacecrafts to let human to know clearly.

Even, space exploration organization also need to let humans to know what are their technical challenges, it will encounter in any space exploration stages to let humans to know. Although, the complexity and changer involved in spaceflight is such for a long time to come there will be a need for experts, whose focus by necessity. So, the general public will know or recognize why it's technical challenges will cause and how it will attempt to solve these technical challenges. It aims to let humans to ensure more than 40 years of spaceflight, the adventive of space, which for technical reasons is inevitably reserved to a " happy few", remains very much the preserve of specialists, cooperation to research how to solve any technical challenges to achieve success in any space exploration mission consequently.

COV19 disease will influence oil price reduces and oil need decreases because many air planes do not need to fly frequently:

Oil price changes influences tourism industry experiences growth life cycle stage or decline life cycle stage. Why is economic theory, a worthwhile thing to do ? e.g. helping organizations to solve challenges, helping society to solve challanges in macro economic view, part of the attraction and the promise of economics is that it cliams to decribe policies that will improve people's lives. This is unlike most other physical and social sciences. Sociology and political science have a policy component, but for the most part, they are concerned with understanding the function of standards of living, but this is really a by-product of science as an intellectual activity matters, physical science, has the potential to improve people standards of living.

What is the role of theory in a policy science? When my view that economic is a policy science. I mean that however either old or new economic theories one useful in policy. Theory is as a substitute for data. For example, we want to determine how a market price will respond to a tax, we could estimate this effect by running a regression of market price, against tax rates, controlling for as many other variable as possible. This would give us an equation that we could use to product how prices respond to change in taxes of one country has many unemployment people, then if it's government change a little 2 to 3 % import tax to private cars. Then, it may cause the country's car buyers number to import car demand decreases. The elastic to car import tax is high because the country has many people are unemployment. Hence, society is continue changing. So, some economists will research how to apply old economic theories to change other new theories to attempt to solve social and organizational challenges.

In new economic theories, they are applied new modelling techniques to old real world problems, they add something to economic knowledge to the extent that we accept formalisation as a source of progress in economic. Some economists focus new economic theory on the dynamic of regional growth and economic activity aspect. When the former foucs on long-run regional growth and later is linked to the " new growth theory". For example, the traditional trade theory is unable to explain the existence of different production structures , e.g. the country's geographical positions in similar regions. Also, trade should lead to conflice face greater market competition and loose incomes. Finally, countries having complementary factors were the best condidates to the formation of trading, so that they will specialize in different commodities. In addition, the traditional trade theory performs poorly when there is high mobility of production factors.

I shall attempt to apply old and new economic theory to explain whether oil changing price has direct relationship to influence global tourism indusry development or tourism income after COVID 19 disease occurs to global below:

Is oil changing price the main to influence tourism income or tourism development or economic growth ? If oil price rises ar falls, it will or won't cause tourism income decreases or increases? If they have cause and effect relationship, what are the main factors to influence tourism income changes by oil price rises or falls ?

I aim to investigate how any why among oil price shocks will influence tourism income variables. We may distinguish between these oil price shocks: Supply-side , aggregate demand and oil specific demand shocks. I assume that oil specific demand shocks affect inflation and the tourism sector equity index. By constrast, I also believe that aggregate demand oil price shock exercisr an effect, either directly and indirectly tourism generated income and economic growth. So, in old economic theory, supply-side , aggregate demand view to oil specific demand shocks will influence tourism income varies. So, governments ought implement strategies against future oil price movements or plan for economic policy development.

In fact, instead of oil price changes will influence tourism income, it could also harm economic growth and tourism activities, due to the effect they expert on transporation, production cost, economic uncertainty.Because tourism activities is one important sector to influence any country's leisure consumption GDP income source. So, sudden fluctations in oil prices may also influence economic growth. It is based a hyphthesis known as the tourism led economic growth. So, it seems that they have direct or indirect relationship to case effect between oil price and tourism activities and development. So, increase on tourism income, the called " economic-driven tourism growth". In addition, high oil prices are affecting certain tourism industry segments , e.g. airlines, cruises lines, hotel, rent travelling car services etc. for oil, importing countries example, with reference to macro economic effects, higher oil prices generally lead to higher inflation, when they negatively influence to country's income.

Hence, from a micro-economic perspective, positive oil price shocks lead to a decline in disposable income. for low income people, it will bring an immediate and negative impact on tourism, mainly due to they feel tourism leisure is regarded as a luxury good, when oil price shocks to rise suddenly . It influences any airline or cruise entertainment service providers' costs are influenced to raise. Then, they need to increase air ticket or cruise ticket price. It will bring on negative tourism leisure demands-side the oil price increases low income group, potential tourism leisure consumers. Hence, it seems that oil price may have indirect relationship to influence tourism leisure consumers' needs.

- How the price of oil changes influences global tourism industry growth or recession?

In macro-economic view, sudden mid and long term oil price shock can influence global torusim industry growth or recession. For example, a oil price of US$180 per barrel was considered only a few years ago, now this has a realistic scenario to which all plaers in the T&T sector have to adapt. At such a high level, the price of oil will become even more critical to almost every part of the tourism value chain. Although, weak global demand, caused by global economic recesson, resulted in a steep oil price decline to US$45 per barrel by the fourth quarter of 2008 in the past low oil price occurrence history, this won't change the mid to long -term oil forecast.

In fact, the past oil price occurrence history of the dramatic structural had changed a high price imposed on airlines, travelers, and destination countries, all of which will have to navigate through times of shifting or even declining travel demand. I assume that a high oil price scenario is assumed in the long term in order to highlight the changes , such a senario would mean for consumer behavior and the competitiveness of several destinations.

Low oil price in the 1970 and early 1980 did not bring significant growth of international air travel, but its growth has been strongest between 1980 and 2004, a period with stable and relatively moderate oil prices. Also, the rapid development of the low-cost carrier business model in the 1990s further fueled air travel growth by capturing tourism leisure demand , such as weekend leisure travel to cities using mostly secondary airports in any big area countries, such as UK, US . However, the tourism growth is whole influenced by high oil prices, due to oil price had been continue rising in possible.

Basis of oil is shortage supply product, oil is assumed to be the main energy source for the aviation sector for the nest 30 years. Although, second-generation biofuels seem to be on the horizon, the economics as well as the production scalability and aviation biofuel shortage will be a main challenge to airline industry. So, I assume that oil price will continue rise up, if there have none any aviation biofuel can be reflected to oil to use for air plane energy.

Until 2004, the only factors to have affected air travel growth, negatively were in external shocks , such as 9/11, causes catching air plane crisis or US regional geopolitical conflicts. It brings some travelers feel fear to go to US travel, as well as until recently 2019, human mouth disease can influence air to have disease to anyone from mouth. So, global travelers number had been continue decreasing, because they are fear to get disease by air when many themselves every stranger travelers are sitting on the without windows air planes. Although, mouth human and air disease and US 9/11 air attack both matters may influence oil price falls effect, because air planes flying times will reduce. They won't need frequent to fly, to cause aviation oil energy need reduce. Consequently, oil price will decrease, due to travelers number reduces and air planes flying times are also influenced to reduce. (oil demand decreases cause oil price decrease). Although, air lines ' cost will also be influenced reduce, but oil price decrease can not bring travelers number increase , when air ticket price reduce because global many leisure and business trip travelers feel fear to catch air planes frequently when human mouth air disease occured in 2019. So, oil price decreases can not grow up tourism industry growth or rise tourism income.

However, the obvious impact of a high oil price is an increase in the operating costs of airline. Moreover, fuel cost as a percentage of airline operating costs vary significantly based on the length of the flight. The longer the flight, the higher the fuel costs as a percentage of the airline operating cost. So, from an online's perspective, long -hauel flights represent the most criticial challenge to profitable operation because the share of fuel on these flights, compared with other cost items, is largest, because of the unfacorable fuel economics, due to fuel costs even at high-load factors. For example, Thai airways dropped its non-stop Bongkok to US flights in the summer of 2008 for commercial reasons, because fuel reached operating cost levels of 55 percent on this route, a cost burden that could not be passed on to their customers. So, the estimated price elacticity of passengers demand at this Bongkok to US flights route is high, if Thai Airways rises less air ticket price, it will influence many travelers to choose other airlines to catch air plan to fly. Hence, due to Thai Airways can not make decision to rise air ticket price, because it believes that it will lose many travelers, so it only chooses to drop this non-stop Bongkok to US flights to avoid fuel cost rising economic loss.

However, although micro and macro economic theories may also that oil price variable or change, it may influence global tourism income. But, recently, on 2019, human mouth and air diseases, it can influence global individual leisure and business trip travelers feel fear to catch air plans to avoid their bodies get this kind of death sickness when they sit in the no fresh air supplying air planes. They feel that they reduce leisure travelling flying times or business trip flying times with strange travelers to sit in crowd air planes together. Then, they must many avoid human moth and air disease to avoid death crisis. Hence, in this global human mouth and air diseases threat environment occurrence, even oil price sudden reduces to low price, it brings airline's cost reduces and air ticke price reduces. However, when air ticket price reduce to be very cheaper, it can not still attract global many leisure or business trip travelers to buy air tickets to fly frequently. Why does air ticket reduction, it can not attract many leisure or businee trip travelers to buy air ticket to fly ? The main reason is because human mouth and air disease influences global many travelers feel fear to catch air planes frequently. In psychological view, this kind of human mouth and air sickness will bring long time negative influence to global traveles do not want to catch air planes for business trips or travelling leisure frequently. So, it implies that oil price changing to influence air ticket price reduction factor ought not main factor to influence tourism income. It may include traveler individual negative emotion psychological factor, such as human mouth and air disease or 2019 9/11 attack both cases, they can influence global travelers feel fear to catch air planes to fly to avoid death threat. So, oil changing price ought not be only one absolute main factor to influence global tourism income significantly.

On conclusion, in economic view, it seems that oil chang price may have indirect or direct relationship to influence tourism income, instead of some unpredicted external environment factors influence, such as US 9/11 attack crisis and human mouth and air disease factors, they may be main factors to influence travellers number to reduce in non-economic external unpredicted environment view. But, in fact, COVID 19 disease may be the main factor to influence global oil need reduces and price reduces .

● How to develop new economic tourism industry after COVID 19 disease disappears ?

How to develop tourism industry in new economic environment? Any examination of the new economic development of travel and tourism requires definitions of the subject and its components, which are suitable for economic analysis. However, in new economic development to tourism industry, it is also important to look at tourism conceptually, in order to set the scene for a deeper understanding of the future new tourism industry development.

Tourism is neither a phenomenon nor a simple set if industries, however, in new or old economic development environment. It is a human activity which encompasses human behavior, use of resources, and interaction with other people, economies and leisure enjoyment environment. It is also involved physical movement of tourists to locales other than their normal living places.

In future new economic environment, traditional travel needs to include these element in order to satisfy traveler enjoyment and leisure feeling: They may include: Tourist needs and motivations, tourism selection and behavior and constraints , travel away from home , market interactions between tourists and those supplying products to satisfy tourist needs and impacts on tourists , hosts, economies and environments.

In new economic environment, the tourism products may include: carriers, in any forms of transport for tourist travel accommodation, man-made attractions, which could also include the managed areas of natural attractions, private sector and public sector support services, middlemen, such as tour wholesalers and travel agents.

The tourism resources may also include: Natural resources, lands , minerals, water and biological; labor resources, human work, and enterprise; capital resources, manmade enhancement and other resources. The travel and tourism resources problems may include: As there is frequently a mismatch between producer and consumer perception of what constitutes the tourism product , there may be conflict in ideas of which resources are properly involved as well as many of the resources likely to be in demand for tourism are public goods , or even free resources.

In new economic development to tourism industry view, we need to consider that tourism and travel has the reputation of being a relatively clean and pleasant industry in which to work or invest in order to attract a greater number of resource suppliers than as less well-perceived industry, which therefore keeps rewards prices down by competition, how to attract those retiring from or travel business for example, if their finances are already sound, income from travel is not expected to be optimal , travel and tourism is frequently highly seasonal , offering rewards that are competitive with other industries only some of the time, destination products are often in locations which are of little use to other industries, so that competition for resource use if minimal and hence rewards are low.

In general, tourist purpose may include: recreational purpose : holiday, health and sport and religion as well as business purpose: company business , e.g. conventions and sales trips. So, in new economic tourism development aim, tourism industry need consider hoe to achieve incentive trips to let these both tourists to feel. For example, the overall type of tourism required, destination arrangement, travel mode, accommodation and attraction visiting and purchasing method or distribution channel. The purchasing method choices may include: whether to buy an inclusive package or separate service, whether to buy direct from suppliers, such as airlines or hotels or use an agent , which tour wholesaler or operate or agent to use.

I predict the tourism development in new economic view, it may have these characteristics: Few enterprises in travel and tourism are large, highly cashed-up and have a large asset base, enterprises within travel and tourism that are not in a financial position to diversify, and those do well success to the above –average growth obtainable in travel and tourism compared with many other industries, they would therefore tend to expand within the sector. The result of individual enterprise growth and integration within travel and tourism is an increase in the concentration of that industry. The degree to which output is produced of fewer and fewer enterprises. This can be only be accounted for realistically with the context of an individual economy, Levels of concentration in any part of travel and tourism in the future are likely to depend on two opposing factors: The constant demand by many tourist market segments for new experiences and products, which encourages the development and survival of more and diverse enterprises, and therefore leads to the reduction of concentration as well as technology, which in travel and tourism frequently calls for large capital outlays and requires mass markets for efficient use, promotes integrations and large scale enterprise, especially in air travel and non-personal services (marketing and information communication, travel insurance , tourism payment methods). IN these areas, concentration will undoubtedly increase in future new economic development environment.

● How new economic development in oil industry after COIV 19 disease

The future global economic growth, it will influence personal incomes and GDP rise. They would carry different weight in different countries at different times. Starting from low levels of incomer and economic development. Household consumption will change from being dominated by basic heat to rapidly rising energy use for higher levels of comfort in space heating and cooling (and large dwellings), and greater use of electrical appliances, finally to a degree of saturation influenced by the income distribution patterns of the country concerned. Income distribution typically changes very slowly, so that the technical market for heart will never be saturated because there will always be a proportion of poor people living in small spaces less comfortably than the average. Industrial energy consumption will be influenced by technical efficiency within each sector, and by changes in the structures of the economy, e.g. changing proportions of agriculture, heavy and light industry, and services. One may eventually see evidence of diminishing marginal returns to additional energy inputs compared to other inputs. Energy consumption in the energy transformation sector may be influenced by income, which drives the demand for electricity to influenced by income, which drives the demand for electricity to grow faster than the demand for heat, but is also subject to the chosen technology of transformation, which is influenced by the cost and availability of primary energy inputs (fuels) in new economic development environment.

IN new economic development environment, it will influences that fuels do not compete in all sectors; for example, the transport sector is dominated by oil. Nuclear and hydroelectric power (and most renewables) reach the user through electricity; electricity itself competes with the direct burning of fossil fuels. Electricity provides the means by which other fuels can compete with oil and gas in sectors, such as space heating and process heat. It also is the only means of powering applications such as motors, computers and lighting: these subsectors are difficult to analyze. However, there is strong evidence that higher incomes do not weaken the demand for electricity so much as the demand for energy in total (in contrast to the effect on the demand for non-electric energy forms).

Econometricians look at the historical record of change in fuel prices and quantities to distinguish several factors between the new economic development and old economic development to oil industry in the future. An income effect. Increasing (reducing) fuel prices reduces (increases) the purchasing power of consumers' income: higher incomes caused by lower prices will increase energy consumption; the consumers' allocation of the increased income to energy purchases may reduce as income rises. Thus income may be heading in a different direction from fuel prices that the effect of fuel price changes when incomes are rising means simply that rising incomes have increased demand. Reducing the cost of using energy through win-win efficiency measures causes a similar problem . On the consequence, in future new economic development environment, it may influence in both cases demand will be less than if the future oil price or efficiency has not changed. The other effect is that an efficiency or substitution effect. An increase in fuel prices may cause consumers to spend more on new equipment, building materials and management operations, which will reduce the amount of fuel required to give the same energy result to the user. The extent of the efficiency effect depends on what happens to the price of the new equipment or building: if those price s rise in line with the fuel price, changes in the balances between fuel and capital or management will not occur. A new user technology , such as the development of the combined cycle gas turbine generator may increase efficiency and thus greatly reduce the quantity of primary fuel needed to produce the required output in this case electricity. If electricity prices had remained sticky, and the electricity and gas markets were not competitive, some of this advantages could have accrued to the gas suppliers in the form of an increase in price, because th4 unit of gas produces more output of electricity, it would have a higher value. In reality, the development of new economic competitive environment in both gas and electricity has tended to ensure that the benefits of such technical advanced accrue to the consumer through lower final prices. The same many apply in the case of improved efficiency in future non-manual driving auto vehicle development: the consumer's cost of motoring is reduced in new economic non-manual driven auto vehicle (Artificial intelligent vehicle) can replace manual driven vehicle , even electricity battery can replace oil energy to be used in vehicles. So, oil price may be influenced to reduce in future new economic development environment.

Airport service life cycle stage improvement strategy can improve future tourism industry to grow up after COVID 19 disease disappears ?
Any organizations will have life cycle stage from birth, growth , mature to decline. In airport service organizations have theis life cycle stages in service aspect. Airports organizatins aim to provide safe, comfortable , even shopping environment to let passengers to stay and to wait to transfer another air planes to visit another destination or arrive the country's airport to check out or check in to enter the airport to leave. If airports have life cycle stages, what the characteristics to every stage? How to improve airport service in order to reach mature life cycle stage rapidly? How to implement airport service strategy in order to reach mature life cycle stage to the aorport organization rapidly?I shall explain as below:
Any airports need to be planned in order to raise excellent service to let passengers to let any travelers choose to travel the country whether the country can provide excellent service and facilities. It will bring indirect emotion impact to influence the travelers chooce to revisit the country to travel again. However, soft or hard element or) staff service performance or airport facility), they will influence whether the different countries travelers to choose to travel to re-visit the country again. So, learning how to keep the mature or airport service life cycle stage to stay long time, it will be one important factor to influence any airport business in success.
In the birth life style stage to airport, airport organizations must maintain the capability to provide expert advice to airport owners an matters including operational safety, during construction, environmental compatibility, and airport development standards. No other private or public organization can be expected maintain this level of proficiency. These value-added services enhance public trust when assuring consistant application of standards for the nation's airport system. So, it seems that when the new airport is built if it hopes its passenger customers can

consider themselves emotion need. So, it ought concentrate on nowadays airplane landing cunways or airport transfer free service transport etc. facilities can let them to feel safe when they were walking in any airport places. If they feel anywhere are dangerous when they are walking or staying in the ne sirport, then new airport non safe or dangerous factor may influence travelers to choose the country to travel again.

Any new airports will need have good new national airport plan in order to it might operate in the near future with respect to safety areas. The plan elements may include as below:

Achieving zero accidents aim, establish standard safety areas at all commercial service airports , achieving the most minimum 85% of all passenger flights operate on runways with safe feeling, increase measure to 100% of all passenger flight operating on runways with standard safety areas after three months. Within 5 years, 95% of all passenger flights begin and end on runways with standard safety areas.

On benefits aspect, aims to mobilize work force to improve safety area performance describes realistic investment benefits. So, in any new airports birth life cycle stage, they must need to consider safety and expenditure for repair aspect in order to keep its service performance to avoid passengers have dissatisfactory feeling when they are staying in their new airports.

When the country has many travelers travel to the country , then the country's new airport passengers number must increase. It is its the new airport growth life cycle stage. These are critical success factors influence the airport, whether it can improve service performance in order to excite different countries travelers visiting the country's airport desire or grow up the visitors number successfully. The critical success factors may include: Having necessary support from internal and externa stakeholders to implement and willing to share information and identify anywhere the total airport facilities of repair needs that are both reliable and feasible projections to let passengers to feel more safe feeling when they are staying in the airport, understand its future service vision and mission, set strategic direction and goals to process/product specific objectives and decision-making across and doen the organization, define, model and prioritize planning prcesses critical for mission performance, practice hand-on sernior management ownership of planning process and allow field, personnel flexiblity in performing jobs, adjust organizational structures , an essessment program to evaluate planning process and product management , e.g. national airport system performance, create organizational understanding of the value management to customer and stakeholder current and future expectations developing human resources management strategies to support new process that solves needs planners and engineers, building information resources strategies change, especially for entering data at the source and maintains data integrity and timeliness.,establish central support group to support reengineering efforts, outreach and training efforts across the organization, phase in short-and long-term results that achieve set goals and objectives over the next two years.

Thus, when one new airport begins to feel passengers number is increasing. It ought experience the growth life cycle stage to the new airport , if it hopes that it can reach mature life cycle stage rapidly as well as keeps its mature life cycle stage to stay in this stage long time or reachs the airport service performance to the most satisfactory level in this mature life cycle stage. It must need to attempt to plan these strategies to implement in order to avoid decline life cycle stage occurs in short time. So, it explains why some new airport can experience the development to mature life cycle stage from grow life cycle stage in short time,even when it reachs mature life cycle stage. It can keep to stay in this stage long time. The reason is that it had prepared effective strategies to achieve how to improve its airport service performance aim in order to satisfy passenger needs. When they are staying in the country's airport any time. Hence, every year revising service performance is needed to any airports.

Any airports must have development processes. The question is that whether the airport needs how long time to reach growth or mature life cycle stage from birth stage or decline life cycle stage will be delayed how long to occur. The development processes may mean that the airport development life cycle stages changes that had toard a particular result or even as a series of continuous actions or operations coducting to an end (Merriam-Webster, 2013).

reference

Merriam-webster (2013). On line dictionary. Available at:
https://www.merriam-webster. com/(last accessed July , 8 2013).

Hence, any airport organizations with experience development pricess. When the new airport is built, it must be in the birth life cycle stage. Its passengers number can not increase rapidly. It needs time to grow their number. But, when the new airport operates a period, many different countries begin feel this new airport is existence in the country. They will attempt to catch airplance to visit this country airport to catch airplane to visit tis country airport to travel. If they feel this country airport service performance can satisfy their short time staying feeling or its passengers or airports visitors number may increase rapidly. It meand that this airport is experiencing growth life cycle stage. So, if the airport can attract many visitors in short time. It will reduce time to growth life cycle stage from birth life cycke stage.

So , service performance may be one important factor to inflow the airport grows. When the airport develops to the period, passengers number can not increase rapidly, it may be the airport's mature life cycle stage. Due to it's passengers number can not grow rapidly, its passengers number also may reduce. When its passengers number has significant decrease, if its reduction number is increasing more. It implies that the airport is experiencing decline life cycle stage. All any country's airport may experience whole life cycle stages. If the country's airport can not implement successful strategies, it may experience birht life cycle stage in long time because it can not grow its passengers number significantly. So, any airports need to learn how to help them to change growth life cycle stage, even mature life cycle stage can stay in long time easily. If they hope to attract many different countries passengers to visit their airports or travel themselves countries or enjoy to stay short time in themselves airports in order to grow themselves airline industry development.

- How can processes improvement management strategy influence airport service performance?

Overall processes in an airport may involve passengers, luggage, cargo, aircraft movements, ground handling, and crews . All of these operations can be systematised into processes at airport terminal. Three main types of processes can be established departing , arrival and transfer . Departure consists in catching a flight to a final or intermediate destination, arrival consists in landing and leaving the airport, and transfer consists in landing at the airport only to catch another flight to a final or an intermediate destination. Airports also deal with cargo. It involves in the movement of cargo by air, cargo fies from the shopper to the consignee through one or more airlines. However, when the airport can let them freight forwarder, being familiar with the necessary procedures how permits the airline to concentrate on the provision of air transport and to avoid time consuming details of the facilitation and landside distribution system. It will raise efficiency and improve service performance. The services product by the ground handling are crucial to the success and efficiency of the airport operations.

These services are usually provided by specialised companies. Briefly, it includes the luggage treatment, passengers carrying from plan to terminal when needed and aircraft assistance. Also, focusing on crew, there are two majoe processes, one for departures and the other for arrivals. The crew members also have to pass the security and passport controls. However, they have special channels for this. Once they reach the aircraft, the similarities with the passengers' procedure stop. Hence, they have to perform a set of activities , such as check the aircraft load sheets and help passengers to name a few. Also airport terminal operations processes for passengers and luggage, typically for departures , passengers do the check on the airline area, pass security controls, proceed to the general lounge and lastly to the gate holding area. arriving passengers are able to immediately go from the luggage claim area, but the non-passengers have to pass the passport control at first. After this passengers have to decide if they need to declare goods or not as the paths are different . Hence, if the airport can reduce all of this service processes are less complex as immigration check in-out service, liggage claim can be efficient to carry when passengers need to find themselves luggage. Then, it will reduce waste time and let they satisfy airport service absolutely. So, reducing service process time amy also help the airport to increase customers number significantly. When airport role is the middleman between airlines , cargo transport service providers and passengers, e.g. short time transport cargo service and reducing passengers check in or check out service time. then, it will let them to feel more satisfactory service to the airport.

Hence, airport capacity is as a multifactor function leaves open the exact relationship between the factors but stresses that all factors are relevant to assess airport capacity . So , understanding airport capacity and what drives the capacity usage at airports may provide an insight in the set of instructments available to optimise the use of capacity. All of these factors may influence any capacity of an airport, they may include as below:

For example, technical constraints, e.g. ATM per hour service in a runway in a combined arrival and departure fashion, when many passengers are staying at the airport, they can withdraw money from ATM easily. So, ATM number facilities service supply number and location choice to the airport factors will infuence passengers ' satisfactory level, another factor is environmental constraints, it can directly offer the wellbeing of the communities surrounding the negative emotion to passengers and communities surrounding the airprt. For this factor, the change in technology and/or operational procedures can provide more capacity in the system.

Airline business models factor, it can affect the capacity spoke model when other under a point-point one ,these models directly affect the peak hour operational capacity, particularly in big international hubs. Airlines often compete with high frequencies between destinations, thus increasing the number of movements. In addition, conncectivity also has downsides for this model: the delays in one airport might be exported and sometimes in another, due to the connectivity influencing the real capacity. This factor has been setting economic incentives or pricing models. Furthermore, expanding information systems, from one airport to multiple airports gate-to-gate concept, and the use of larger airport to redcuce frequencies.

Hence, above these factors may influence whether the airport needs how long time to reach maturiry life cycle stage when it is staying the growth life cycle stage. It depends on how its strategies implementation and how environment influence its implementation , if it hopes to achieve to reach the maturity life cycle stage in success in short time.

Finally, I shall explain life cycle cst analysis to any country pavement strategy will bring what significant influential benefits to any airports continue to develop in order to avoid to reach decline life cycle stage time in short time easily , when they are staying in the mature life cycle stage. In the construction or rehabilitation investments of highway's pavements, it is already common to perform a life-cycle analysis or life cycle cost analysis for different alternatives to airport pavements. Becauae when any airport pavements are using for a long time, every day has many airplanes need to fly to land on the pavement. It can bring significant repace influence when the airport has many airplanes are needed to land on the pavements every day in the maturity life cycle stages.

Hence, how to evaluate the repair cost expenditure budget in order to satisfy every day air planes land on the airport pavement need. In the calculations are different cost factors (including direct and indirect cost)to any airport itself pavement. Direct costs are related to the critical construction cost landing on pavement activities and are calculated with information from the airport agency and constructors that work for them. The indirect costs are related with the loss of daily revenue of the airport during work activities, such as landing on the airport pavement.

Runways are the most critical pavements area of airport , so it is critical to ensure the quality of these pavement to let airplanes to land on the airport safety, e.g. they need to be constructed with sufficient strength to carry the moving airport and have a high resistance to skidding and aquaplaining. It is most of the time accomplished with reconstructions or deep rehabilitation. Hence, predicting how much will spend on airport pavement facilities expenditure must need in every day.

However, the life cycle assessment (LCA) is a mult step procedure for calculating the life time environmental impact of a product or service is needed to any airport organizations, when they reachs maturity life cycelt stage . The complex process includes goal and cope definition in inventory analysis impact assessment. The process is vaturally iteractive as quality and completeness of information is constantly being testes. When the definition of the aim and scope of the study is done the next step is the development of an inventory, in which all significant environmental burdens during the lifetime of the product,, such as airport pavements or process , such as airplanes landing on the pavement or airplanes leaving from the pavement in the airport.

(Araujo, Oliveria & Silve) 2014 explained that life cycle snslysis of pavements are focused on the activities of extraction, production, transportation application of materials, concisely the construction of the road. Because its difficult to obtain other relevant data knowing that the use phase of the pavement is predominant with repect to energy consumption and also to gas emissions related to the atmosphere. One of the main factors for the use phase is the rolling resistance, this depends on the surface and structural characteristics of the different pavements.

Hence, , if the airport can have good repairment or renew skills to help its pavement to improve. Then, it may bring long time benefit, such as reducing airplanes energy consumption and also to avoid gas emissions or reduce gas emissions accident occurrene, even air plane landing on pavement accident occurrence chance can reduce to the zero. so, defining the expected pavement performance time improvement strategy can influence whether the airport pavement can satisfy all airplane users how long time landing on or leaving on the airport pavement. Also it is the major factor to influence airport main function success for any airplanes arriving to the country's airport pavement or leaving from the country's airport pavement. Hence, calculating any airport pavement life cycle costs factor. It is necessary to analysis and interpret carefully the results to identfy the most economic pavement strategy in any airport's whole life cycle development stages.

reference

Araujo, J.P.C. Oliveria, J.R.M. & Silva H.M.R.D. (2011) . the importance of the use phase on the LCA of environmentally friendly solutions for asphalt road pavements. transportation research part D: trasport and environment, 32(0), 97-110. Retrieved in March 2015 from:// dx. doi.org/10.1016/j.trd.2014.07.006.

CHAPTER FOUR

How COVID 19 disease influences cruise leisure need

In fact, the cruise and air tourism leisure activiites are very similar, travellers will be influenced to bring negative emotion when they need to travel on the cruise or catch air planes to go to another country o travel by COVID 19 disease influence. The COVID-19 pandemic has a huge impact on the tourism industry due to the resulting travel restrictions as well as slump in demand among travelers. The tourism industry has been massively affected by the spread of coronavirus, as many countries have introduced travel restrictions in an attempt to contain its spread. The United Nations World Tourism Organization estimated that global international tourist arrivals might decrease by 58% to 78% in 2020, leading to a potential loss of US$0.9–1.2 trillion in international tourism receipts. In many of the world's cities, planned travel went down by 80–90%. Conflicting and unilateral travel restrictions occurred regionally and many tourist attractions around the world, such as museums, amusement parks, and sports venues closed. UNWTO reported a 65% drop in international tourist arrivals in the first six months of 2020. Air passenger travel showed a similar decline. So, it seems that COVID 19 disease may influence cruise passengers number decrease.

How COVID 19 disease influences cruise pasengers their tourism leisure on sea to Singapre and Australia cruise leisure passengers number and insurance medical expenses to cruise passenger are raised ?

I shall indicate Caribban ship in Singapore case example as below:

A Royal Caribbean ship in Singapore that had been forced to turn around after reporting a positive case of COVID-19, has confirmed the passenger did not actually have the virus. Singaporean officials confirmed to CNN this week that the 83-year-old man who tested positive reported a false positive test.

Following protocol after the initial news of his testing positive earlier this week, fellow passengers in close contact with him were placed under quarantine and the crew began a contact tracing process. The quarantined passengers will be compensated for the days of travel they missed, the cruise line told CNN. "We have rescinded the Quarantine Orders of his close contacts, who had earlier been placed on quarantine as a precautionary measure while investigations were ongoing," Royal Caribbean said in a statement.

This was the ship's third sailing since it resumed "ocean getaway voyages" with no port calls. The ship, which was operating at 50% capacity, had left Singapore on Dec. 7 and was in its second day of sailing when the supposed case was discovered, Cruise Critic reported.

Passengers and crew who are not considered close contacts with the thought to be infected guest (1,679 passengers and 1,148 crew) remained on the ship and were allowed to disembark and were not forced to isolate. In order to board the ship, passengers were required to test negative for COVID-19 within three days of the start of the trip and wear a contact tracing-enabled wristband while on board. Only Singapore residents were allowed to board.

The cruise line relaunched sailings in Singapore, but has cancelled most of its planned itineraries elsewhere through Feb. 28. And while Royal Caribbean is looking for volunteers to test new health protocols in the U.S. (part of the Centers for Disease Control and Prevention's 'Conditional Sail' Order), it was not immediately clear when those would take place.

Royal Caribbean isn't alone in trying to resume sailings only for those efforts to be stymied by an outbreak of the virus on board. SeaDream Yacht Club restarted sailings in the Caribbean last month, but was forced to turn around when several passengers and crew tested positive for coronavirus. Thus, it seems that COVID 19 disease may influencce Singapore cruise lesiure destination passengers number decreases.

As a result of the pandemic, many countries and regions have imposed quarantines, entry bans, or other restrictions for citizens of or recent travellers to the most affected areas. Other countries and regions have imposed global restrictions that apply to all foreign countries and territories, or prevent their own citizens from travelling overseas.Together with a decreased willingness to travel, the restrictions have had a negative economic impact on the travel sector in those regions. A possible long-term impact has been a decline of business travel and international conferencing, and the rise of their virtual, online equivalents.Concerns have been raised over the effectiveness of travel restrictions to contain the spread of COVID-19.

For how COVID 19 disease influences Australia cruise industry example, tourism bodies have suggested that the total economic cost to the sector, as of 11 February 2020, would be A$4.5 billion. Casino earnings are expected to fall. At least two localities in Australia, Cairns and the Gold Coast, have reported already lost earnings of more that $600 million.The Australian Tourism Industry Council (ATIC) called on the Government of Australia for financial support especially in light of the large number of small businesses affected. In March, national travel agency Flight Centre has indefinitely closed 100 stores throughout Australia, due to significantly lower demand for travel.It also suffered a 75% decline in share price, and announced that 6,000 staff would be made redundant or placed on unpaid leave globally.

On the 781-foot vessel's Promenade deck, an art gallery abuts a big-screen movie theater. The Lido deck has a fitness center and full-service spa.

That cornucopia of amenities has greeted guests on largely smooth sailings over the past 20 years. But by late March, the vessel had been transformed into an isolation ward, and by the time the ship finally docked in Florida in early April, four passengers had died, two of whom had been diagnosed with Covid-19.

The cruise industry, which the Cruise Lines International Association says was worth $150 billion worldwide in 2018, is now assessing the damage. Even as the coronavirus continues to spread, though, some key industry players are already seeing signs of growth in the coming years. A cruise industry resurgence would send thousands back to work and send travelers back to sunny ports across the globe. While some cruisers are eager to book, other tentative travelers have concerns about their health, medical emergencies and their money.

Can COVI19 disease cause the cruise industry service staffs lose jobs?

In a quarterly report released on April 3, Carnival Corporation, the world's largest travel leisure company, predicted that the coronavirus impact could be grave.

"We have never previously experienced a complete cessation of our cruising operations," the report reads, noting the high costs of repatriating passengers, assisting quarantined crew and the possibility of lawsuits related to the corporation's handling of the pandemic. Wedbush analyst James Hardiman recently estimated Carnival was burning $500 million in cash reserves each month.

But Carnival stock -- which by March 18 had dropped over 82% from a high in mid-January -- got a boost when Saudi Arabia officials announced on April 6 that the country's sovereign wealth fund had acquired an 8% stake in the company.

How cruise travelers can protect themselves ?

Given the ongoing risk of coronavirus, some cruisers are looking to travel insurance as a way to ensure their medical treatment would be covered if they contract the illness. While coverage varies between companies and policies, Scott Adamski, head of US field sales for AIG Travel, wrote in an emailed statement that many standard plans cover onboard treatment from the ship's doctor, treatment at port or transport to another medical facility. Medical evacuation, which can be very expensive when paid out of pocket, is also covered by some plans. That evacuation could range from commercial flights with a medical-provider escort to an air ambulance; Adamski stressed the importance of learning the details of an individual plan before making a purchase. In the wake of the coronavirus crisis, thousands of cruisers have looked to companies for refunds or credits. Most cruise lines have offered flexible policies around cancellation and rebooking amid the pandemic.

But as travel industry struggles to cope with the disruption, some are wondering what will happen if future bookings are canceled as well. Travel insurance can help, but as with health issues, the details of individual plans vary widely.

Travel insurance would likely not cover travelers if the cruise company cancels the cruise, according to Adamski. Travelers, he notes, should contact the cruise company for a refund or voucher. (Another option Adamski suggests is to contact your credit card company, which may have some provisions for cancellations of trips you booked on the card.)

For example, if a traveler decides to cancel a cruise because of their own concerns about coronavirus, Adamski believes that a refund via travel insurance is unlikely. Covered reasons for cancellation are listed in individual policies, and generally include things such as medical emergencies and weather events. Hence, cruise lesiure companies need to help cruise passengers to buy health and medical insurance to avoid their compensation loss , due to COVD19 disease can attack any one passenger when he/she goes on the cruise to travel in the cruise travelling days, e.g. one week, one month, even, three months or more times. So, when any one cruise passenger spends long time to stay on the cruise, he/she will get the COVID 19 disease easily when he/she needs to contact to any one cruise staff, e.g. cleaner, restaurant waiter, crew, even cruise passenger. Hence, COVID 19 disease may also influence many cruise passengers feel fear to choose cruise to travel, even they won't decide to stay long time on the cruise. Consequently, they may be influenced by COVID 19 disease either shortening cruise time to week, short cruise journey or canceling any cruise journeys easily.

On conclusion, air and cruise travellers will be influenced to reduce travelling leisure activities, even air ticket and cruise ticket prices are decreasing by COVID 19 disease. Also, it implies that COVD 19 disease may be the most influential factor to compare economic recession, pollution, inflation, unemployment rate rising etc. factors to reduce future travellers number in global.

CHAPTER FIVE

Illness how influences Economic Recession

COVID 19 disease how influences consumer individual visiting shopping behavior

As the virus swept the globe, brands changed how they interacted with customers due to social distancing and stay-at-home orders. Consumer buying patterns also shifted with fluctuations in the stock market, skyrocketing unemployment and supply chain issues. As many people lost their jobs and those still earning a paycheck worried about future layoffs, impulse purchasing became infrequent. Messages that resonated with consumers a few weeks prior suddenly fell flat and even seemed insensitive.

In the early weeks of the pandemic response, many brands implemented a crisis marketing strategy, pivoting messaging and offers as quickly as possible. Hotels.com shifted ads with its mascot, Captain Obvious, from partying with friends to eating popcorn alone with a bottle of hand sanitizer. Panera launched Panera Grocery, enabling customers to buy high-demand grocery items it already stocks in its restaurants—such as bread, produce and milk—along with soups and sandwiches. In an effort to help parents with kids at home full time, Time for Kids magazine gave anyone access to its 2020 digital editions for free, and Amazon Prime provided kids with free video content.

COVID 19 disease can influence consumers need to attempt to adapt to new virtual consumption behaviors

As stay-at-home and social distancing orders took hold in the spring, customers relied even more heavily on digital and mobile platforms as their smartphones became a lifeline to the outside world. New virtual behaviors emerged and expanded as consumers completed their daily tasks digitally, such as curbside pickup, telehealth appointments, online workouts and contact-free delivery. And as many people worked from home, went to school online, and connected with family and friends virtually, video chat use exploded. The video chat platform Zoom saw a staggering 418% growth in adoption rate in two just months. In response to these new behaviors, brands proactively showed customers how they fit into new routines and expectations. Pizza Hut rolled out tamper-proof seals, making it apparent if anyone has opened a pizza box before it gets to the intended destination. Beauty brand MAC created a tool to let customers virtually try on lipstick and eye shadow since they could no longer sample colors at a makeup counter or MAC store.

How coronavirus impacts consumer behavior

Consumer needs are changing as a result of the pandemic. The way people interact with brands—and how they view themselves as consumers—is fundamentally different than it was pre-quarantine. Spicer has seen three major shifts in consumer buying habits:

Home: People are spending more time in their homes, which has both practical and emotional effects. A conversation Spicer had with Samsung centered on how people are rethinking the role that products such as home appliances now play. Not only do appliances need to work, but people have other considerations as well, such as: Is my washing machine quiet enough to have a Zoom call in the next room? Does the vacuum clean deep enough to remove germs? Where are appliance materials sourced from?

By quickly adding online lessons to its product offerings, Guitar Center took advantage of the national mindset of setting goals for self-improvement projects during stay-at-home orders. Through social media and email, the retailer stayed in contact while encouraging people to make music at home. And for those not quite yet ready to learn new chords, Guitar Center shared musical videos of popular, professional guitar players for inspiration.

Consumer shopping habits and behavior shift constantly, but in pre-COVID times, brands could normally pivot on smaller scales to make a difference—like offering gluten-free options or making content available on streaming platforms. Coming out of the pandemic, people are thinking about their role as consumers differently, which will force brands to make larger fundamental changes to anticipate new consumer needs.

Physically, people are now on devices and networks that weren't previously commingled—such as work computers on home IP addresses. Additionally, more individuals in the house are on those Wi-Fi networks across devices, making unique identification complicated. More existentially, people are craving relationships and connection. They're likely not expecting brands to fill that need, but any brand that does will be rewarded for its efforts.

"COVID-19 is going to affect the platforms you use, the content you create, the offers you design and campaigns to support those offers," Solis says. "Essentially, you have the opportunity to start from scratch and build those touchpoints, hopefully investing heavily in artificial intelligence and machine learning across the journey."

Because COVID-19 impacts consumers differently across states and geographic areas, brand marketers should carefully think through how a range of consumers will react. How will your campaign play in big cities like Atlanta or New York and in smaller towns in rural areas? And how do you shift the messaging based on location?

Concern over health and safety, especially personal contact and large groups, will likely remain with us for months and possibly years. While some pre-COVID-19 behaviors will return at some point, many of the changes that occurred during the pandemic are likely to become permanent, especially new habits like video chats with family, telehealth visits with doctors and virtual workouts at home.

Brands should look to build their infrastructure and future products to support this likely permanent shift to using virtual platforms and options when possible. Even without mandatory social distancing guidelines, many consumers will continue to favor online activities due to the convenience factor.

The cornerstone of marketing has always been creating connections with customers. The pandemic created a new world where relationships with both people and brands became more important than ever. By closely monitoring ever-shifting customer sentiment and priorities, and leveraging tools to ramp up personalization, businesses can leave the crisis with new long-term customers.

COVID 19 disease may bring below negative visiting shopping emotion influence to global consumers

New global consumer research shows how consumers are radically changing their lives in response to the pandemic. Many consumers are facing new personal situations, with changes in income and leisure time, which are influencing attitudes and behaviors. Consumers are shopping with greater awareness of the environment, health and cost, favoring locally-sourced products and neighborhood stores. The huge rise in digital commerce, especially among new or low-frequency consumers, is likely to continue post-pandemic.

Retail consumer behavior is changing at unprecedented speed

The COVID-19 global pandemic is having a profound impact on consumers' lives. As stay-at-home orders and country-wide lockdowns start to be eased, consumer behavior continues to be driven by new personal circumstances, such as changes in discretionary income and spare time, and reconsidered values and priorities.

Retail consumers adapt to new personal circumstances

Changes to disposable income and available leisure time are influencing consumers' attitudes, behaviors and purchasing habits. For example, 33% of consumers are finding themselves 'financially-squeezed', with less disposable income compared to before the crisis, and are shopping more cost consciously, whereas 26% (the 'Resource-Rich') have increased both their disposable income and free time, and are enjoying new leisure pursuits.

In markets where the pandemic is stabilizing, economic concerns remain high, denting consumer confidence. And although fears about health are gradually subsiding, consumers remain uncomfortable about visiting public places, although they are relatively more comfortable with familiar places such as grocery and pharmacy stores.69% of consumers in stabilizing markets and 80% in advancing markets are fearful for the health of others

Retail consumers adopt conscious and mindful purchasing habits

Consumers are more mindful than ever about what they are buying—and it's a mindset that's likely to continue. The majority (75%) are limiting food waste, and 67% are shopping more health-consciously. In both cases, 90% of these consumer groups are likely to continue with these habits.

Demand for local goods is growing, as consumers seek out products they feel they can trust, and efficiency is also on consumers' minds, as they are doing fewer and larger shopping trips. Overall, there are 10 consumer trends impacting goods purchased. 64% of consumers agree that governments and businesses will increase their focus on the environment.

Retail consumers embrace digital commerce and omnichannel

With lock-downs in place and many stores shuttered, ecommerce has surged. Adoption has accelerated from previously uninitiated users, especially in under-penetrated categories such as grocery. Consumers have also increased their use of omnichannel services like contactless payment, social commerce, virtual consultations and curbside pickup. It's new behavior that they plan to continue.

Retail consumers find creative ways to fill their time at home

With more time spent at home, consumers are engaging in new or renewed activities during their spare time. More than half (62%) are trying new recipes, 51% are spending time on home improvements, and 48% are embarking on new skills or online education. In each case, the vast majority expect to continue with these activities.

Families are welcoming the opportunity to spend more time together, and new ways of socializing are gaining in popularity as people connect virtually. With the switch in many cases to working from home, employees have embraced their new environments and many expect to continue or increase their time spent home working in the future.

Consequently, the retail industry has experienced major disruptions in the past, but consumer preferences and shopping patterns have never shifted so quickly. As well as changing how they shop, the reasons why consumers shop has also changed forever. Retailers need to draw on data-driven insights to renew their relationship with consumers.

Responsibility to employees and consumers has taken on a new significance. When it comes to restarting the economy, the near-ubiquitous lack of consumer confidence will pose an enormous challenge. Retailers need to build trust with consumers, such as implementing visible safety and hygiene measures for staff and customers in stores.

COVID 19 disease how brings online shopping
behavior chance

The huge rise in digital commerce, especially among new or low-frequency consumers, is likely to continue post-pandemic.Nowadays,

COVID 19 disease had influence global visiting shop consumers choose to buy any products from online. I shall indicate US online shopping development trend example as below:

Months into the coronavirus disease 2019 (COVID-19) pandemic, Americans' online shopping habits are continuing to shift. We documented changes in online shopping habits at the beginning of the pandemic, comparing patterns from January and February (before the pandemic) with patterns from mid-March and April (when lockdowns and other restrictions were beginning).

We now present findings from an August 2020 RAND American Life Panel (ALP) survey, in which we followed up with approximately 1,900 of our original respondents. In this survey, we asked respondents how often they shopped online in July and August. This survey reflects not only how often people are shopping online and whether they are spending more or less on online shopping, but how shopping behaviors have (or have not) changed since the early days of the COVID-19 pandemic.

We have divided our respondents into three categories on the basis of how often they shop online: frequent (once a week or more), occasional (a few times a month) and infrequent (never or almost never) online shoppers.

In January and February, our respondents were roughly equally split between these categories, as Figure 1 shows. This pattern changed substantially: Online shopping became more common as COVID-19 spread. This change has persisted as the pandemic continues. By August, about 45 percent of our respondents were frequent, one-third were occasional, and only one-quarter were infrequent online shoppers.

By summer 2020, overall trends in online shopping had substantially changed, although these changes were by no means universal. The frequency of online shopping has continued to increase; frequent online shoppers have risen from 35 to 45 percent of all shoppers, even as 55 percent of respondents stuck with their prepandemic habits. Forty percent of our respondents were spending more money online, even as 20 percent were spending less. These trends reinforce what other data show: Although many households have been able to pivot to working and shopping from home, some of those in less-fortunate circumstances are cutting back.

In the August ALP survey, also asked respondents to estimate whether the amount of money that they had spent on online purchases had gone up or down since February. Specifically, we asked respondents whether their spending had doubled, increased by a smaller amount, stayed about the same, or decreased. We cannot calculate exactly how much more or less households are spending, but these responses do provide some sense of changes at the household level.

Thirty-nine percent of Americans reported that they had increased their online spending—11 percent estimated that they had doubled their spending and 28 percent estimated that they had increased it by a smaller amount. Forty-three percent reported spending about the same amount of money, and 19 percent reported spending less.

Unsurprisingly, people who said that they shopped online more frequently were generally spending more on online purchases, although the pattern is not clear-cut. Of those who were shopping online more in July and August, about half were also spending more money. About 42 percent said that their spending had not changed, and 9 percent said that it actually had decreased. Among people who were doing the same amount of online shopping or were shopping online less often, 32 to 35 percent were spending more and about 25 percent were spending less. (ALP surveys, Mayn and Aug. 2020).

SOURCE: Authors' calculations using 1,883 responses in the ALP surveys that were conducted in May and August 2020.

NOTE: Respondents were asked the following question: "Over the past month, how often did you do online shopping or get home delivery of any products, including meals, groceries, medication, clothing, books, or other products?" Responses are weighted using sampling weights, as described in Carman and Nataraj, 2020.

Thus, it implies that COVD 19 disease had influenced many US consumers choose to buy any products from online. US Household income seems to be related to spending on online shopping, although perhaps not in the expected direction. Households earning less than $40,000 were more likely to decrease their online spending than higher-income households since March, but they were also most likely to double their online spending within the same time period. It is possible that these households are still spending less in total dollar value than other households, even if they have doubled their spending.

Bibliography

Carman, Katherine Grace, and Shanthi Nataraj, 2020 American Life Panel Survey on Impacts of COVID-19: Technical Documentation, Santa Monica, Calif.: RAND Corporation, RR-A308-1, 2020. As of November 2,

2020: https://www.rand.org/pubs/research_reports/RRA308-1.html
——, 2020 American Life Panel Survey on Impacts of COVID-19: May 2020 Survey Results, Santa Monica, Calif.: RAND Corporation, RR-A308-2-v2, 2020. As of November 2, 2020: https://www.rand.org/pubs/research_reports/RRA308-1.html
——, 2020 American Life Panel Survey on Impacts of COVID-19: August 2020 Survey Results, Santa Monica, Calif.: RAND Corporation, RR-A308-8, 2020. As of November 2, 2020: https://www.rand.org/pubs/research_reports/RRA308-1.html
Cohen, Patricia, Ben Casselman, and Gillian Friedman, "An Extra $600 a Week Kept Many Jobless Workers Afloat. Now What Will They Do?" New York Times, July 29, 2020, updated September 10, 2020.

Thus, COVID 19 disease had influene the global buying habits of shoppers tend to change slowly. Covid-19, however, has been disruptive enough to shake them up, and companies are trying to take advantage.
global businesses need to bring all creatures of habit, and shopping is largely habit-driven. There are very few times in one's life when you have an opportunity to reshape their habits. The classic three are when you get married, when you move home and when you have a baby. And otherwise, your habits are pretty cemented, and you're not really open to forming new habits. And so what this current moment has created is a moment when everyone's habits are up for grabs.

What Is the Risk of Getting COVID-19 While Shopping in order to bring online shopping chance raises?

Whether the shopping is indoors or outdoors, with outdoors being safer the number of people shopping — fewer means it's easier to maintain social (physical) distancing how long you'll take — the faster you're done, the better COVID-19 positivity rate in the local community. So, global many consumers had felt online shopping is more safe to compare to visit shops by COVID 19 disease influence.

The impact of online grocery shopping on food consumer behavior in Covid-19. Some researchers Uses bivariate probit models to empirically investigate the impact of online purchasing channels on Chinese urban consumer food hoarding behaviors with random survey samples. Some research results show that fresh food e-commerce channels are more likely to be associated with panic stockpile behaviors due to higher likelihood of supply shortages than offline channels with government assistance in logistic management. In contrast, community group buy, another format of e-commerce, appears superior in satisfying the consumer needs and easing the panic buying perception.

It suggests that online channels may have diverse impacts on consumers' panic stockpiling behaviors during the extreme situations. Online channels need to develop efficient supply chains to be more resilient to extreme situations and the government shall recognize the increasing share of the online channels together with traditional offline channels when implementing supporting policies. With ever increasing share of online channels, it is imperative in terms of policy implications to understand how would online channels affect hoarding behavior.

Originality/value

They are the first study in online shopping's impact on food stockpile during pandemics using a random sample. Although food stockpile behavior at times of emergency have been investigated in many literature, there are no empirical studies on the impact of online channels on stockpile behaviors under extreme situations. Unlike disasters that immediately impact every entity in supply chains covering producers, vendors, distribution centers and retailers, pandemics did not render supply chains affected immediately, but rather increase consumers' willingness to shop online to avoid virus. Thus, Covid-19 provides a natural experiment to investigate the online channels' impact on stockpile behavior. So, COVID 19 disease may influence many consumers choose to buy foods from online channel.

The situation is rapidly changing. The amount of people deemed safe to gather in a single place has dwindled from thousands, to hundreds, to ten. Restaurants, bars, movie theaters, and gyms in many major cities are shutting down. Meanwhile many office workers are facing new challenges of working remotely full time.

Essentially, people are coming to terms with the realities of our interconnected world and how difficult it is to temporarily separate those connections to others. To say that we are living in unprecedented times feels like an understatement.

One of the responses we've seen to how people are approaching this period of isolation and uncertainty is in huge overnight changes to their shopping behaviors. From bulk-buying to online shopping, people are changing what they're buying, when, and how.

As more cities are going under lockdowns, nonessential businesses are being ordered to close, and customers are generally avoiding public places. Limiting shopping for all but necessary essentials is becoming a new normal. Brands are having to adapt and be flexible to meet changing needs.

This resource is intended to provide information so that you can make the best decisions for your brand during uncertain times. We've gathered some facts and numbers around how behaviors are changing, what products people are buying, and what industries are feeling the strain to help you determine what choices you can make for your business.

Understanding Panic Buying and Coronavirus

As news of COVID-19 spread and as it was officially declared a pandemic by the World Health Organization, people responded by stocking up. They bought out medical supplies like hand sanitizer and masks and household essentials like toilet paper and bread. Soon, both brick-and-mortar and online stores were struggling to keep up with demand, and price gouging for supplies became rampant.

Humans respond to crises in different ways. When faced with an uncertain, risky situation over which we have no control, we tend to try whatever we can to feel like we have some control.

Paul Marsden, a consumer psychologist at the University of the Arts London was quoted by CNBC as saying: "Panic buying can be understood as playing to our three fundamental psychology needs." These needs are autonomy (or the need to feel in control of your actions), relatedness (the need to feel that we are doing something to benefit our families), and competence (the need to feel like smart shoppers making the correct choice).

These psychological factors are the same reasons "retail therapy" is a response to many different types of personal crises; however, during a pandemic there are added layers.

One is that the global spread of COVID-19 has been accompanied by a lot of uncertainty and at times contradictory information. When people are hearing differing advice from multiple sources, they have a greater instinct to over-, rather than under-, prepare.

Secondly, there is the crowd mentality. Seeing other people buying up the shelves and then seeing a scarcity of necessary products validates the decision to stock up. No one wants to be left behind without any resources.

Understanding the COVID-19 Effect on Online Shopping Behavior

Get The Print Version

Tired of scrolling? Download a PDF version for easier offline reading and sharing with coworkers.

I don't think it's too soon to say that the COVID-19 global pandemic will likely be one of the defining events of 2020, and that it will have implications that last well into the decade.

The situation is rapidly changing. The amount of people deemed safe to gather in a single place has dwindled from thousands, to hundreds, to ten. Restaurants, bars, movie theaters, and gyms in many major cities are shutting down. Meanwhile many office workers are facing new challenges of working remotely full time.

Essentially, people are coming to terms with the realities of our interconnected world and how difficult it is to temporarily separate those connections to others. To say that we are living in unprecedented times feels like an understatement.

One of the responses we've seen to how people are approaching this period of isolation and uncertainty is in huge overnight changes to their shopping behaviors. From bulk-buying to online shopping, people are changing what they're buying, when, and how.

As more cities are going under lockdowns, nonessential businesses are being ordered to close, and customers are generally avoiding public places. Limiting shopping for all but necessary essentials is becoming a new normal. Brands are having to adapt and be flexible to meet changing needs.

This resource is intended to provide information so that you can make the best decisions for your brand during uncertain times. We've gathered some facts and numbers around how behaviors are changing, what products people are buying, and what industries are feeling the strain to help you determine what choices you can make for your business.

Understanding Panic Buying and Coronavirus

As news of COVID-19 spread and as it was officially declared a pandemic by the World Health Organization, people responded by stocking up. They bought out medical supplies like hand sanitizer and masks and household essentials like toilet paper and bread. Soon, both brick-and-mortar and online stores were struggling to keep up with demand, and price gouging for supplies became rampant.

Humans respond to crises in different ways. When faced with an uncertain, risky situation over which we have no control, we tend to try whatever we can to feel like we have some control.

Paul Marsden, a consumer psychologist at the University of the Arts London was quoted by CNBC as saying: "Panic buying can be understood as playing to our three fundamental psychology needs." These needs are autonomy (or the need to feel in control of your actions), relatedness (the need to feel that we are doing something to benefit our families), and competence (the need to feel like smart shoppers making the correct choice).

These psychological factors are the same reasons "retail therapy" is a response to many different types of personal crises; however, during a pandemic there are added layers.

One is that the global spread of COVID-19 has been accompanied by a lot of uncertainty and at times contradictory information. When people are hearing differing advice from multiple sources, they have a greater instinct to over-, rather than under-, prepare.

Secondly, there is the crowd mentality. Seeing other people buying up the shelves and then seeing a scarcity of necessary products validates the decision to stock up. No one wants to be left behind without any resources.

COVID-19 is Changing the Ecommerce Landscape.

Retail businesses around the world over are being affected by COVID-19 through everything from rapidly changing customer behavior to supply issues.

We're offering a snapshot of the data around these changes and how businesses are adapting to them.

Read the Infographic

Is it Safe to Order Online During COVID-19?

As it becomes even more clear just how infectious COVID-19 is, some shoppers have raised questions about the safety of receiving their online orders. Experts are finding that the virus can live on surfaces from three hours to up to three days, depending on the material. (Note that conclusive findings are difficult to come by in these early days of the virus, and as experts continue their study of it, these numbers may change.)

That said, it's unlikely that COVID-19 would survive on your purchased items from the time they were packed to the time you received your package (especially with the slowdown in the delivery system). And shipping conditions make a tough environment for COVID-19 as well, so it's not likely you'll be exposed via the package itself, either.

According to the CDC, "[T]here is likely very low risk of spread from products or packaging that are shipped over a period of days or weeks at ambient temperatures." The CDC's statement refers to packages that have been in shipment for at least several days and did not come into contact with any sources of contamination after packaging.

The World Health Organization addresses the concern as well, by saying that it is safe to receive packages from locations with reported COVID-19 cases. From their website: "The likelihood of an infected person contaminating commercial goods is low and the risk of catching the virus that causes COVID-19 from a package that has been moved, travelled, and exposed to different conditions and temperature is also low."

Generational Purchasing Responses to COVID-19

The response to COVID-19 hasn't been universally felt across generations, with consumers of different age groups responding differently to the crisis.

It is important to caveat that this is a rapidly evolving situation so surveys are quickly outdated as behaviors change with the circumstances. This applies to data shared here and below.

1. Gen Z and Millenials.

While people in general are concerned about the growing pandemic, the youngest generations are particularly altering their purchasing behaviors.

One survey of U.S. and U.K. consumers found that 96% of Millenials and Gen Zs are concerned about the pandemic and its effects on the economy. This concern is leading them to change their behavior more dramatically than other generations, which includes cutting back on spending, stocking up on items, and spending less on experiences.

2. Gen X and Boomers.

Although still concerned about coronavirus and its effects on the economy, older generations are slightly less concerned than younger generations and letting it impact their shopping habits less. For example, 24% of Boomers and 34% of Gen X said they were letting current events impact what items they purchase, compared to nearly half of Millennials.

COVID-19: Men's and Women's Shopping Behaviors Vary

While data shows that shopping behaviors are changing based on generational differences, we're also seeing variations based on gender.

While survey data shows that women are more likely to be concerned about the effects of COVID-19, it also shows that men are more likely to have it impact their shopping behaviors. One-third of men, compared to 25% of women, reported the pandemic affecting how much they spend on products. Additionally, 36% of men, compared to 28% of women, reported it affecting how much they are spending on experiences (travel, restaurants, entertainment, etc.).

Men were also found to be shopping online and avoiding in-store experiences more than women. This includes taking advantage of options that limit in-store interactions like BOPIS (buy online, pick-up in store), curbside pickup, and subscription services.

Changes in Revenue Across Ecommerce

As people have embraced social distancing as a way to slow the spread of the pandemic, there has naturally been a drop-off in brick-and-mortar shopping. That would seem to mean there would likely be an increase in online shopping as people turn to ecommerce to purchase the items they might have otherwise purchased in person.

Has that prediction won out? In reality, ecommerce sales are not higher across the board, although some industries are seeing significant upticks. This is especially true for online sellers of household goods and groceries. JD.com, China's largest online retailer, has seen sales of common household staples quadruple over the same period last year. A survey by Engine found that people are spending on average 10-30% more online.

1. Grocery ecommerce.

Grocery ecommerce soared in the second week of March, after shoppers turned online to find the goods they needed but weren't available at their local grocery stores. The following graph, with data from Rakuten Intelligence, shows a huge spike in grocery-related ecommerce. The rest of ecommerce seems like it might be up a little bit, but no drastic peaks or valleys.

2. Other ecommerce categories.

In addition to grocery, ecommerce covers a wide number of products, across categories. Common Thread Collective has been providing valuable updates with COVID data on ecommerce shopping behavior, including the chart below. While ecommerce performance is not generally up or down, breaking down the data by vertical tells a bit more of the story.

Understanding the COVID-19 Effect on Online Shopping Behavior

Get The Print Version

Tired of scrolling? Download a PDF version for easier offline reading and sharing with coworkers.

I don't think it's too soon to say that the COVID-19 global pandemic will likely be one of the defining events of 2020, and that it will have implications that last well into the decade.

The situation is rapidly changing. The amount of people deemed safe to gather in a single place has dwindled from thousands, to hundreds, to ten. Restaurants, bars, movie theaters, and gyms in many major cities are shutting down. Meanwhile many office workers are facing new challenges of working remotely full time.

Essentially, people are coming to terms with the realities of our interconnected world and how difficult it is to temporarily separate those connections to others. To say that we are living in unprecedented times feels like an understatement.

One of the responses we've seen to how people are approaching this period of isolation and uncertainty is in huge overnight changes to their shopping behaviors. From bulk-buying to online shopping, people are changing what they're buying, when, and how.

As more cities are going under lockdowns, nonessential businesses are being ordered to close, and customers are generally avoiding public places. Limiting shopping for all but necessary essentials is becoming a new normal. Brands are having to adapt and be flexible to meet changing needs.

This resource is intended to provide information so that you can make the best decisions for your brand during uncertain times. We've gathered some facts and numbers around how behaviors are changing, what products people are buying, and what industries are feeling the strain to help you determine what choices you can make for your business.

Understanding Panic Buying and Coronavirus

As news of COVID-19 spread and as it was officially declared a pandemic by the World Health Organization, people responded by stocking up. They bought out medical supplies like hand sanitizer and masks and household essentials like toilet paper and bread. Soon, both brick-and-mortar and online stores were struggling to keep up with demand, and price gouging for supplies became rampant.

Humans respond to crises in different ways. When faced with an uncertain, risky situation over which we have no control, we tend to try whatever we can to feel like we have some control.

Paul Marsden, a consumer psychologist at the University of the Arts London was quoted by CNBC as saying: "Panic buying can be understood as playing to our three fundamental psychology needs." These needs are autonomy (or the need to feel in control of your actions), relatedness (the need to feel that we are doing something to benefit our families), and competence (the need to feel like smart shoppers making the correct choice).

These psychological factors are the same reasons "retail therapy" is a response to many different types of personal crises; however, during a pandemic there are added layers.

One is that the global spread of COVID-19 has been accompanied by a lot of uncertainty and at times contradictory information. When people are hearing differing advice from multiple sources, they have a greater instinct to over-, rather than under-, prepare.

Secondly, there is the crowd mentality. Seeing other people buying up the shelves and then seeing a scarcity of necessary products validates the decision to stock up. No one wants to be left behind without any resources.

COVID-19 is Changing the Ecommerce Landscape.

Retail businesses around the world over are being affected by COVID-19 through everything from rapidly changing customer behavior to supply issues.

We're offering a snapshot of the data around these changes and how businesses are adapting to them.

Read the Infographic

Is it Safe to Order Online During COVID-19?

As it becomes even more clear just how infectious COVID-19 is, some shoppers have raised questions about the safety of receiving their online orders. Experts are finding that the virus can live on surfaces from three hours to up to three days, depending on the material. (Note that conclusive findings are difficult to come by in these early days of the virus, and as experts continue their study of it, these numbers may change.)

That said, it's unlikely that COVID-19 would survive on your purchased items from the time they were packed to the time you received your package (especially with the slowdown in the delivery system). And shipping conditions make a tough environment for COVID-19 as well, so it's not likely you'll be exposed via the package itself, either.

According to the CDC, "[T]here is likely very low risk of spread from products or packaging that are shipped over a period of days or weeks at ambient temperatures." The CDC's statement refers to packages that have been in shipment for at least several days and did not come into contact with any sources of contamination after packaging.

The World Health Organization addresses the concern as well, by saying that it is safe to receive packages from locations with reported COVID-19 cases. From their website: "The likelihood of an infected person contaminating commercial goods is low and the risk of catching the virus that causes COVID-19 from a package that has been moved, travelled, and exposed to different conditions and temperature is also low."

Generational Purchasing Responses to COVID-19

The response to COVID-19 hasn't been universally felt across generations, with consumers of different age groups responding differently to the crisis.

It is important to caveat that this is a rapidly evolving situation so surveys are quickly outdated as behaviors change with the circumstances. This applies to data shared here and below.

1. Gen Z and Millenials.

While people in general are concerned about the growing pandemic, the youngest generations are particularly altering their purchasing behaviors.

One survey of U.S. and U.K. consumers found that 96% of Millenials and Gen Zs are concerned about the pandemic and its effects on the economy. This concern is leading them to change their behavior more dramatically than other generations, which includes cutting back on spending, stocking up on items, and spending less on experiences.

2. Gen X and Boomers.

Although still concerned about coronavirus and its effects on the economy, older generations are slightly less concerned than younger generations and letting it impact their shopping habits less. For example, 24% of Boomers and 34% of Gen X said they were letting current events impact what items they purchase, compared to nearly half of Millennials.

COVID-19: Men's and Women's Shopping Behaviors Vary

While data shows that shopping behaviors are changing based on generational differences, we're also seeing variations based on gender.

While survey data shows that women are more likely to be concerned about the effects of COVID-19, it also shows that men are more likely to have it impact their shopping behaviors. One-third of men, compared to 25% of women, reported the pandemic affecting how much they spend on products. Additionally, 36% of men, compared to 28% of women, reported it affecting how much they are spending on experiences (travel, restaurants, entertainment, etc.).

Men were also found to be shopping online and avoiding in-store experiences more than women. This includes taking advantage of options that limit in-store interactions like BOPIS (buy online, pick-up in store), curbside pickup, and subscription services.

Changes in Revenue Across Ecommerce

As people have embraced social distancing as a way to slow the spread of the pandemic, there has naturally been a drop-off in brick-and-mortar shopping. That would seem to mean there would likely be an increase in online shopping as people turn to ecommerce to purchase the items they might have otherwise purchased in person.

Has that prediction won out? In reality, ecommerce sales are not higher across the board, although some industries are seeing significant upticks. This is especially true for online sellers of household goods and groceries. JD.com, China's largest online retailer, has seen sales of common household staples quadruple over the same period last year. A survey by Engine found that people are spending on average 10-30% more online.

1. Grocery ecommerce.

Grocery ecommerce soared in the second week of March, after shoppers turned online to find the goods they needed but weren't available at their local grocery stores. The following graph, with data from Rakuten Intelligence, shows a huge spike in grocery-related ecommerce. The rest of ecommerce seems like it might be up a little bit, but no drastic peaks or valleys.

2. Other ecommerce categories.

In addition to grocery, ecommerce covers a wide number of products, across categories. Common Thread Collective has been providing valuable updates with COVID data on ecommerce shopping behavior, including the chart below. While ecommerce performance is not generally up or down, breaking down the data by vertical tells a bit more of the story.

3. Subscription services.

While ecommerce sales do not generally appear to be skyrocketing as one might expect, there are some exceptions. One of these is in subscription and convenience services, which have seen significant upward trends in both revenue and conversion.

Product Categories Shifting During COVID-19

As people are making buying choices based on new and ever-changing global and local circumstances, the product categories that are being purchased are also changing.

Market research company Nielsen has identified six key consumer behavior thresholds tied to the COVID-19 pandemic and their results on markets.

These are:

Proactive health-minded buying (purchasing preventative health and wellness products).

Reactive health management (purchasing protective gear like masks and hand sanitizers).

Pantry preparation (stockpiling groceries and household essentials).

Quarantine prep (experiencing shortages in stores, making fewer store visits).

Restricted living (making much fewer shopping trips, limited online fulfillment).

A new normal (return to daily routines, permanently altered supply chain).

As we progress through these stages, the items people choose to buy and the product categories that thrive continue to change. Here are some of the product categories most affected.

1. Health and safety products.

Anyone who has faced empty shelves or seen price gouging online knows that health and safety products are being purchased far faster than they can be produced and restocked.

According to data from Nielsen, items like hygienic and medical mask sales are up by more than 300%.

2. Shelf-stable goods.

Another category of consumer packaged goods that is booming is shelf-stable items. These fit into the category of people planning for long-term quarantine. According to Nielsen, products like shelf-stable milk and milk substitutes (particularly oat milk) are up by more than 300% in dollar growth. Other items seeing increases are things like dried beans and fruit snacks that have a long shelf life.

3. Food and beverage.

In addition to long-term quarantine type items, for groceries in general, sales are up. However, there are some behavioral changes around the way people are buying groceries.

For example, in an effort to avoid crowds at supermarkets, many people are choosing BOPIS (buy-online-pick-up-in-store) or delivery options. Downloads of apps like Instacart and Shipt that allow people to hire personal shoppers to prepare and in some cases deliver their grocery orders have increased by between 124% (for Shipt) and 218% (for Instacart). People are also choosing to buy these items from online stores more than they did prior.

Shipbob, a shipping and fulfillment partner for ecommerce stores, gathered data from 3,000+ of their merchants and is tracking the data. While the chart below shows some fluctuations, the month-over-month increase in online sales for food and beverage is 18.8%

4. Digital streaming.

While less about the immediacy of protecting and feeding themselves, it comes as no surprise that as people are homebound and no longer pursuing external entertainment options that there is an increase in digital streaming services. In addition to streaming services like Netflix, Amazon, Hulu, and Disney+ seeing atypical gains in subscribers in the first quarter of 2020, non-traditional streaming services like movie studios are releasing media streaming, on-demand, sometimes earlier than projected release.

5. Luxury goods.

While the above products and services are increasing in sales due to the current situation, other industries are not doing as well. In addition to obvious ones like entertainment, restaurants, and travel, one area projected to have significant losses is the luxury goods industry.

Vogue Business projects a potential loss as great as $10 billion for this industry in 2020 due to COVID-19. This is in part because luxury goods rely heavily on the Asian market's purchasing power, where the pandemic has been affecting consumers since January.

Understanding the COVID-19 Effect on Online Shopping Behavior

Get The Print Version

Tired of scrolling? Download a PDF version for easier offline reading and sharing with coworkers.

I don't think it's too soon to say that the COVID-19 global pandemic will likely be one of the defining events of 2020, and that it will have implications that last well into the decade.

The situation is rapidly changing. The amount of people deemed safe to gather in a single place has dwindled from thousands, to hundreds, to ten. Restaurants, bars, movie theaters, and gyms in many major cities are shutting down. Meanwhile many office workers are facing new challenges of working remotely full time.

Essentially, people are coming to terms with the realities of our interconnected world and how difficult it is to temporarily separate those connections to others. To say that we are living in unprecedented times feels like an understatement.

One of the responses we've seen to how people are approaching this period of isolation and uncertainty is in huge overnight changes to their shopping behaviors. From bulk-buying to online shopping, people are changing what they're buying, when, and how.

As more cities are going under lockdowns, nonessential businesses are being ordered to close, and customers are generally avoiding public places. Limiting shopping for all but necessary essentials is becoming a new normal. Brands are having to adapt and be flexible to meet changing needs.

This resource is intended to provide information so that you can make the best decisions for your brand during uncertain times. We've gathered some facts and numbers around how behaviors are changing, what products people are buying, and what industries are feeling the strain to help you determine what choices you can make for your business.

Understanding Panic Buying and Coronavirus

As news of COVID-19 spread and as it was officially declared a pandemic by the World Health Organization, people responded by stocking up. They bought out medical supplies like hand sanitizer and masks and household essentials like toilet paper and bread. Soon, both brick-and-mortar and online stores were struggling to keep up with demand, and price gouging for supplies became rampant.

Humans respond to crises in different ways. When faced with an uncertain, risky situation over which we have no control, we tend to try whatever we can to feel like we have some control.

Paul Marsden, a consumer psychologist at the University of the Arts London was quoted by CNBC as saying: "Panic buying can be understood as playing to our three fundamental psychology needs." These needs are autonomy (or the need to feel in control of your actions), relatedness (the need to feel that we are doing something to benefit our families), and competence (the need to feel like smart shoppers making the correct choice).

These psychological factors are the same reasons "retail therapy" is a response to many different types of personal crises; however, during a pandemic there are added layers.

One is that the global spread of COVID-19 has been accompanied by a lot of uncertainty and at times contradictory information. When people are hearing differing advice from multiple sources, they have a greater instinct to over-, rather than under-, prepare.

Secondly, there is the crowd mentality. Seeing other people buying up the shelves and then seeing a scarcity of necessary products validates the decision to stock up. No one wants to be left behind without any resources.

COVID-19 is Changing the Ecommerce Landscape.

Retail businesses around the world over are being affected by COVID-19 through everything from rapidly changing customer behavior to supply issues.

We're offering a snapshot of the data around these changes and how businesses are adapting to them.

Read the Infographic

Is it Safe to Order Online During COVID-19?

As it becomes even more clear just how infectious COVID-19 is, some shoppers have raised questions about the safety of receiving their online orders. Experts are finding that the virus can live on surfaces from three hours to up to three days, depending on the material. (Note that conclusive findings are difficult to come by in these early days of the virus, and as experts continue their study of it, these numbers may change.)

That said, it's unlikely that COVID-19 would survive on your purchased items from the time they were packed to the time you received your package (especially with the slowdown in the delivery system). And shipping conditions make a tough environment for COVID-19 as well, so it's not likely you'll be exposed via the package itself, either.

According to the CDC, "[T]here is likely very low risk of spread from products or packaging that are shipped over a period of days or weeks at ambient temperatures." The CDC's statement refers to packages that have been in shipment for at least several days and did not come into contact with any sources of contamination after packaging.

The World Health Organization addresses the concern as well, by saying that it is safe to receive packages from locations with reported COVID-19 cases. From their website: "The likelihood of an infected person contaminating commercial goods is low and the risk of catching the virus that causes COVID-19 from a package that has been moved, travelled, and exposed to different conditions and temperature is also low."

Generational Purchasing Responses to COVID-19

The response to COVID-19 hasn't been universally felt across generations, with consumers of different age groups responding differently to the crisis.

It is important to caveat that this is a rapidly evolving situation so surveys are quickly outdated as behaviors change with the circumstances. This applies to data shared here and below.

1. Gen Z and Millenials.

While people in general are concerned about the growing pandemic, the youngest generations are particularly altering their purchasing behaviors.

One survey of U.S. and U.K. consumers found that 96% of Millenials and Gen Zs are concerned about the pandemic and its effects on the economy. This concern is leading them to change their behavior more dramatically than other generations, which includes cutting back on spending, stocking up on items, and spending less on experiences.

2. Gen X and Boomers.

Although still concerned about coronavirus and its effects on the economy, older generations are slightly less concerned than younger generations and letting it impact their shopping habits less. For example, 24% of Boomers and 34% of Gen X said they were letting current events impact what items they purchase, compared to nearly half of Millennials.

COVID-19: Men's and Women's Shopping Behaviors Vary

While data shows that shopping behaviors are changing based on generational differences, we're also seeing variations based on gender.

While survey data shows that women are more likely to be concerned about the effects of COVID-19, it also shows that men are more likely to have it impact their shopping behaviors. One-third of men, compared to 25% of women, reported the pandemic affecting how much they spend on products. Additionally, 36% of men, compared to 28% of women, reported it affecting how much they are spending on experiences (travel, restaurants, entertainment, etc.).

Men were also found to be shopping online and avoiding in-store experiences more than women. This includes taking advantage of options that limit in-store interactions like BOPIS (buy online, pick-up in store), curbside pickup, and subscription services.

Changes in Revenue Across Ecommerce

As people have embraced social distancing as a way to slow the spread of the pandemic, there has naturally been a drop-off in brick-and-mortar shopping. That would seem to mean there would likely be an increase in online shopping as people turn to ecommerce to purchase the items they might have otherwise purchased in person.

Has that prediction won out? In reality, ecommerce sales are not higher across the board, although some industries are seeing significant upticks. This is especially true for online sellers of household goods and groceries. JD.com, China's largest online retailer, has seen sales of common household staples quadruple over the same period last year. A survey by Engine found that people are spending on average 10-30% more online.

1. Grocery ecommerce.

Grocery ecommerce soared in the second week of March, after shoppers turned online to find the goods they needed but weren't available at their local grocery stores. The following graph, with data from Rakuten Intelligence, shows a huge spike in grocery-related ecommerce. The rest of ecommerce seems like it might be up a little bit, but no drastic peaks or valleys.

Source

2. Other ecommerce categories.

In addition to grocery, ecommerce covers a wide number of products, across categories. Common Thread Collective has been providing valuable updates with COVID data on ecommerce shopping behavior, including the chart below. While ecommerce performance is not generally up or down, breaking down the data by vertical tells a bit more of the story.

Source: Common Thread Collective

3. Subscription services.

While ecommerce sales do not generally appear to be skyrocketing as one might expect, there are some exceptions. One of these is in subscription and convenience services, which have seen significant upward trends in both revenue and conversion.

Performance branding company WITHIN has been tracking the effects of COVID-19 on ecommerce across a number of specific sectors by monitoring and comparing data from select businesses year-over-year. This graph comes from their observations:

Subscription services chart

Source: WITHIN

Product Categories Shifting During COVID-19

As people are making buying choices based on new and ever-changing global and local circumstances, the product categories that are being purchased are also changing.

Market research company Nielsen has identified six key consumer behavior thresholds tied to the COVID-19 pandemic and their results on markets.

These are:

Proactive health-minded buying (purchasing preventative health and wellness products).

Reactive health management (purchasing protective gear like masks and hand sanitizers).

Pantry preparation (stockpiling groceries and household essentials).

Quarantine prep (experiencing shortages in stores, making fewer store visits).

Restricted living (making much fewer shopping trips, limited online fulfillment).

A new normal (return to daily routines, permanently altered supply chain).

As we progress through these stages, the items people choose to buy and the product categories that thrive continue to change. Here are some of the product categories most affected.

1. Health and safety products.

Anyone who has faced empty shelves or seen price gouging online knows that health and safety products are being purchased far faster than they can be produced and restocked.

According to data from Nielsen, items like hygienic and medical mask sales are up by more than 300%.

Health and safety products chart

2. Shelf-stable goods.

Another category of consumer packaged goods that is booming is shelf-stable items. These fit into the category of people planning for long-term quarantine. According to Nielsen, products like shelf-stable milk and milk substitutes (particularly oat milk) are up by more than 300% in dollar growth. Other items seeing increases are things like dried beans and fruit snacks that have a long shelf life.

3. Food and beverage.

In addition to long-term quarantine type items, for groceries in general, sales are up. However, there are some behavioral changes around the way people are buying groceries.

For example, in an effort to avoid crowds at supermarkets, many people are choosing BOPIS (buy-online-pick-up-in-store) or delivery options. Downloads of apps like Instacart and Shipt that allow people to hire personal shoppers to prepare and in some cases deliver their grocery orders have increased by between 124% (for Shipt) and 218% (for Instacart).

People are also choosing to buy these items from online stores more than they did prior.

Shipbob, a shipping and fulfillment partner for ecommerce stores, gathered data from 3,000+ of their merchants and is tracking the data. While the chart below shows some fluctuations, the month-over-month increase in online sales for food and beverage is 18.8%

4. Digital streaming.

While less about the immediacy of protecting and feeding themselves, it comes as no surprise that as people are homebound and no longer pursuing external entertainment options that there is an increase in digital streaming services. In addition to streaming services like Netflix, Amazon, Hulu, and Disney+ seeing atypical gains in subscribers in the first quarter of 2020, non-traditional streaming services like movie studios are releasing media streaming, on-demand, sometimes earlier than projected release.

5. Luxury goods.

While the above products and services are increasing in sales due to the current situation, other industries are not doing as well. In addition to obvious ones like entertainment, restaurants, and travel, one area projected to have significant losses is the luxury goods industry.

Vogue Business projects a potential loss as great as $10 billion for this industry in 2020 due to COVID-19. This is in part because luxury goods rely heavily on the Asian market's purchasing power, where the pandemic has been affecting consumers since January.

6. Fashion and apparel.

As mentioned above, omnichannel sellers are seeing big losses, in part because they're closing the retail arms of their businesses all together. People are understandably not interested in shopping for clothes in person. Department stores like Macy's and JCPenney, large chains like Abercrombie & Fitch and Nike, and DTC brands with some storefronts like Rothys and Everlane are all closing their physical stores and experiencing losses. Some stores like Patagonia are halting even their online stores to protect all workers in their supply chain.

Even online apparel sales are down as people are putting more of their budgets into daily essentials. The chart below is again from Shipbob's data of their 3,000+ merchants. This shows an overall 20% decrease in sales month-over-month.

COVID 19 disease how impacts global economic recession on shopping aspect

The COVID-19 pandemic has had far-reaching economic consequences beyond the spread of the disease itself and efforts to quarantine it. As the SARS-CoV-2 virus has spread around the globe, concerns have shifted from supply-side manufacturing issues to decreased business in the services sector. The pandemic caused the largest global recession in history, with more than a third of the global population at the time being placed on lockdown. Supply shortages are expected to affect a number of sectors due to panic buying, increased usage of goods to fight the pandemic, and disruption to factories and logistics in mainland China. There have been instances of price gouging.There have been widespread reports of shortages of pharmaceuticals, with many areas seeing panic buying and consequent shortages of food and other essential grocery items.The technology industry, in particular, has been warning about delays to shipments of electronic goods.

By COVID 19 disease influences to global economy losses, Economic recovery programmes are began to implement by EU countries

Some economic recovery programmes include Next Generation EU and Pandemic Emergency Purchase Programme. A study published in August 2020 concluded that the direct effect of the response to the pandemic on global warming will likely be negligible and that a well-designed economic recovery could avoid future warming of 0.3 °C by 2050. The study indicates that systemic change for "decarbonization" of humanity's economic structures is required for a substantial impact on global warming, which also has economic aspects. Beyond targeted financing of green projects or sectors, contemporary decision-making mechanisms also allow for excluding projects with substantial environmental, social, or climate risks from financial relief. Over 260 civil society organizations called on Chinese actors to ensure that COVID-19 related Belt and Road Initiative funding excludes such projects.In November 2020 the IMF said that governments and central banks had promised $19.5 trillion of support since the coronavirus began.

Food crisis on agricultural aspect influences by COVID 19 disease

In food crisis countries, up to 80 percent of the population relies on agriculture for their livelihoods. Therefore, any further disruptions to food production and related value chains, for example in the form of reduced availability of critical inputs or restricted access to lands or markets, could be catastrophic for vulnerable populations.The agriculture sector plays an important role in influencing migratory patterns. Transhumant pastoral populations are likely to be hard hit by any border closures, as they rely on seasonal movements of livestock for their food and income. The disruption of traditional and western patterns and the creation of new ones may lead to tensions and even violent conflicts between resident and pastoralist communities, resulting in local displacement and increased levels of poverty and food insecurity.

According to FAO, it is crucial to maintain and support the continuous functioning of local food markets, value chains and agri-food systems in food crisis contexts, including through ongoing and scaled up support to food processing, transport, marketing, and so forth; strengthening of local producers' groups to maintain negotiation power and access to markets; and, advocating for trade corridors to remain open as much as possible during COVID-19 related movement restrictions.

COVID 19 diease how influences global financial market

Economic turmoil associated with the coronavirus pandemic has wide-ranging and severe impacts upon financial markets, including stock, bond and commodity (including crude oil and gold) markets. Major events included the Russia–Saudi Arabia oil price war that resulted in a collapse of crude oil prices and a stock market crash in March 2020. The United Nations Development Programme expects a US$220 billion reduction in revenue in developing countries, and expects COVID-19's economic impact to last for months or even years.[46][30] Some expect natural gas prices to fall.

COVID 19 hoe influences global manufacturing

New vehicle sales in the United States have declined by 40%. The American Big Three have all shut down their US factories. The German automotive industry came into the crisis after having already suffered from the Dieselgate-scandal, as well as competition from electric cars. Boeing and Airbus suspended production at some factories. A survey conducted by the British Plastics Federation (BPF) explored how COVID-19 is impacting manufacturing businesses in the United Kingdom (UK). Over 80% of respondents anticipated a decline in turnover over the next 2 quarters, with 98% admitting concern about the negative impact of the pandemic on business operations.

Impact of the COVID-19 pandemic on the arts and cultural heritage, entertainment and sport lesiure industry

The epidemic had a sudden and substantial impact on the arts and cultural heritage (GLAM) sectors worldwide. The global health crisis and the uncertainty resulting from it profoundly affected organisations' operations as well as individuals – both employed and independent – across the sector. By March 2020, across the world most cultural institutions had been indefinitely closed (or at least with their services radically curtailed) exhibitions, events and performances cancelled or postponed. Many individuals temporarily or permanently lost contracts or employment with varying degrees of warning and financial assistance available. Equally, financial stimulus from governments and charities for artists, have provided greatly differing levels of support, depending on the sector and the country. In countries such as Australia, where the arts contributed to about 6.4% of GDP, effects on individuals and the economy have been significant.

The impact of COVID 19 disease how influences global cinema entertainment industry

The pandemic has impacted the film industry. Across the world and to varying degrees, cinemas have been closed, festivals have been cancelled or postponed, and film releases have been moved to future dates. As cinemas closed, the global box office dropped by billions of dollars, while streaming became more popular and the stock of Netflix rose; the stock of film exhibitors dropped dramatically. Almost all blockbusters to be released after the March opening weekend were postponed or cancelled around the world, with film productions also halted. Massive losses in the industry have been predicted.

The impact of COVD 19 disease infuences to television and video game entetainment industry, they have similar consumer behavior , this disease excits many young and old age audiences choose to watch movies at homes and young age people choose to buy video game to play at homes.

The COVID-19 pandemic has shut down or delayed production of television programs in several countries.[citation needed] However, a joint report from Apptopia and Braze showed a 30.7% increase in streaming sessions worldwide on platforms such as Disney+, Netflix, and Hulu during the month of March.

The pandemic also affected the video game sector to a smaller degree. As the outbreak appeared in China first, supply chains affected the manufacturing and production of some video game consoles, delaying their releases and making current supplies scarcer. As the outbreak and pandemic spread, several keystone trade events, including E3 2020, were cancelled over concerns of further spread. The economic impact on the video game sector is not expected to be as large as in film or other entertainment sectors as much of the work in video game production can be decentralised and performed remotely, and products distributed digitally to consumers regardless of various national and regional lockdowns on businesses and services.

How CVID 19 disease influences publish industry, it influences many readers choose to read e-books from home computer, they do not like to visit book shops to buy books.

In light of the public health situation in which includes afflicted regions where retail sectors deemed non-essential have been ordered closed for the interim, Diamond Comic Distributors announced on 24 March 2020 a full suspension of distributing published material and related merchandise as 1 April 2020 until further notice. As Diamond has a near-monopoly on printed comic book distribution, this is described as an "extinction-level event" that threatens to drive the entire specialized comic book retail sector out of business with that one move. As a result, publishers like IDW Publishing and Dark Horse Comics have suspended publication of their periodicals while DC Comics is exploring distribution alternatives including an increased focus on online retail of digital material.

COVID 19 disease influences online shopping has more customers global.
The pandemic has impacted the retail sector. Shopping centres around the world responded by reducing hours or closing down temporarily. As of 18 March 2020, the footfall to shopping centres fell by up to 30%, with significant impact in every continent.Additionally, product demand exceeded supply for many consumables, resulting in empty retail shelves.In Australia, the pandemic has provided a new opportunity for daigou shoppers to re-sell into the China market.
Some retailers have employed contactless home delivery or curbside pickup for items purchased through e-commerce sites.By April, retailers had started implementing "retail to go" models where consumers could pick up their orders. An estimated 40% of shoppers were shopping online and

choosing to pick up in-store, a behavior that had suddenly doubled as compared to the previous year.

Small-scale farmers have been embracing digital technologies as a way to directly sell produce, and community-supported agriculture and direct-sell delivery systems are on the rise. For Amazon ecommerce example, it help Amazon increases many online consumers. Many traditional visiting shops consumers began to choose to apply internet channel to buy any products. In mid-April, Amazon confirmed that workers at over half of its 110 U.S. warehouses had been diagnosed with coronavirus.On 16 June, the United States Department of Commerce announced that retail sales for the month of May had seen an increase of 17.7% from April as states began to reopen and lift restrictions. According to CNBC, This marks the biggest one month jump in the history of retailing in the United States. Numbers for June reflected a 7.5 percent rise in sales. So, it causes many shops close, due to many visting shop customers began to accept to apply internet or online channel to buy any products to replace visiting shops purchase method.

Hence, instead of COVID 19 disease influences tourism recession, it also brings many shops close, but it creates new online purchase model to excite many traditional visiting shop purchase consumers began to choose online purchase model in retail aspect. But it also influences many restaurants close, because many people feel fear to go to restaurants to eat, due to food environment may be one most serious COVID 19 disease places. So, many people choose to buy food to cook at home, so, supermarkets may be one attractive place to let us to choose to buy food more safe to compare restaurants. Thus, COVID 19 disease may cause some kinds of businesses close , but it also bring new chance to some kinds of businesses.

When economy recovers after COVID disease disappears

Firstly, we need to know how Long Does Immunity Last After COVID-19? Then, we can analyze whether when global economy may recover in possible when COVID 19 disease can disappear in future one day. For those who recover from COVID-19, new research shows immunity to the virus can last for at least 8 months, and may last much longer. Understanding how our immune system responds to the virus is an important step in vaccine development. Currently two vaccines, from Pfizer-BioNTech and Moderna, are authorized for use in the United States. Several other promising vaccines are also in development, but until they become widely available we must practice physical distancing and mask-wearing to keep transmission down.

Since the start of the COVID-19 pandemic, there's been a push to develop and roll out a vaccine against the SARS-CoV-2 virus.

If scientists and health professionals can do that quickly, and while we slow the spread of the disease, it's believed that we can limit deaths by achieving herd immunity.

While scientists have been working hard on many fronts to understand the virus and develop controls for it, there's still much we don't know about immunity after recovery from COVID-19, including how long it lasts.

Knowing how long immunity lasts is important in creating vaccination protocols.

How Quickly Can the Economy Recover From COVID-19?

The current economic situation is unprecedented—never before has an industrialized economy intentionally shut down.

While the suddenness and severity of the downturn is alarming, the scale of the federal response has been commensurate.

Past recessions were followed by relatively slow recoveries, but the COVID-19 rebuilding era may be more similar to the period following a large natural disaster.

Falling from a high point: The economy entered 2020 in an extraordinarily well-balanced position. And unlike previous recessions, no structural imbalances currently stand in the way of a rapid recovery.

Going into 2020, the economic expansion was on solid footing. Inflation was running just shy of the Federal Reserve's long-term two percent target, implying a sustainable level of aggregate demand.

Unemployment had reached a 50-year low and the economy was running very close to its maximum potential.

For example, in 2008, the housing bubble burst, destroying trillions of dollars in wealth and creating a wave of bad debt.

This caused consumer demand to crater and lending standards to tighten.

The lengthy rebalancing process created a tremendous amount of labor market slack.

The economy in 2008 could not simply "snap back" to its prior condition—dislocations from the housing bubble had to be absorbed before sustainable growth could resume.

Nearly a decade of above-trend growth was required for the economy to

rebound at full strength.
The recovery from COVID-19 in 2020 may be different—there are no structural imbalances that need to be rectified before the economy can begin rebuilding.

A commensurate federal response: to indicate that when US economy may recover when COVID 19 disease disappeared. A self-enforced shutdown has placed the economy in a holding pattern. Never before has the labor market contracted so rapidly. But the CARES Act has helped soften the blow.

Approximately 26 million Americans have been laid off since the coronavirus outbreak began, with weekly unemployment claims spiking to record highs in the first weeks of April.
The Bureau of Economic Analysis estimates that US GDP contracted at a 4.8 percent annualized pace in the first quarter, but this period only includes the first weeks of the shutdown in March. Second-quarter figures, which include data for April and May, will better represent the severity of the shutdown.
Fortunately, Congress has responded to the crisis with an unprecedented aid package that may help small businesses retain nearly 60 million employees until the economy is able to reopen.
In coming weeks, we are likely to see that many of the millions who were unemployed in early April before the help from the two-month grant provided by the Cares Act reached the small business community will go back on the books of their previous jobs (that is be counted as employed).]
By allowing shuttered businesses to keep worker on the books, the Paycheck Protection Program (PPP) may accelerate the recovery and decrease the drag that typically accompanies rehiring.
The PPP incentivizes business owners to bring their out-of-work employees back on the payroll.
In another innovative wrinkle, unemployment insurance benefits have increased and expanded to cover 10 million freelance workers through the summer. This should help sustain consumer demand through the downturn.
Despite worries that more generous benefits might deter workers from returning to the job, the relief funding is timed to expire in eight weeks when large parts of the economy are expected to reopen.

a natural disaster recovery: Instead of gradually rebalancing and rebuilding demand over a period of years, the economy may rapidly recover from the COVID-19 shutdown. The process of reopening may be similar to the rebuilding period that follows a major natural disaster.

The US may experience a disruption similar to what the Gulf Coast region went through after Hurricane Katrina in 2005.

Businesses emerged from the storm in stages; some essential contractors began operating within days, while the hospitality and tourism sectors required years to rebound.

With the support of an intact financial system and federal relief programs, the New Orleans metro economy was relatively quick to rebound. The city's GDP growth paused in 2005 but returned to its pre-disaster trajectory by 2006.

Of course, there are major differences between COVID-19 and Hurricane Katrina. The COVID-19 damage is not confined to a local region, and the disruptions from social distancing may persist to some degree for years.

On the other hand, there has been no damage to the nation's physical capital—there will be no need to wait for construction and cleanup once it is safe to reopen.

How Fast Can the U.S. Economy Recover From COVID-19?

We expect U.S. GDP to fall 5.1% in 2020. This is far worse than the Great Recession. Before jumping to pessimistic conclusions, however, investors should consider a much more important issue: What is the recovery going to look like? We expect robust catch-up growth in the years following 2020. By 2024, we think that the U.S. GDP level will recover to just 1% below our pre-COVID-19 expectation.

Our analysis of the history of global recessions showed that many recessions don't have a long-run negative impact on the economy. The worst recessions in terms of long-run impact (the Great Depression or the Great Recession) are generally the product of persistent economic policy error. But economic policy response has been extremely impressive so far in 2020, especially the United States' historically large fiscal stimulus.

Fiscal stimulus is already lifting up U.S. economic activity substantially. Stimulus provided a massive boost to personal disposable incomes in April. Though much of the extra income was saved, more detailed analysis shows that the stimulus payments still boosted spending. Meanwhile, the extra savings means that household and firm balance sheets will be in good shape to spend more as the economy recovers.

We expect broad availability of a vaccine to erase COVID-19's direct impact on the U.S. and global economies by mid-2021. The need to social distance will continue to weigh heavily on some parts of the economy (with the hardest-hit constituting about 5% of GDP) through the rest of 2020. However, positive data about the vaccine's efficacy should arrive in the second half of 2020, bolstering consumer and business confidence and promoting a broader recovery in the economy.

U.S. Can Mount Solid Recovery in Second Half Even as COVID-19 Drags Highly on Some Sectors

We think a crucial perspective in modeling the near-term trajectory of the U.S. economy is to look at the industry level, as different industries are seeing disparate impact from the pandemic. We group U.S. industries into three broad categories based on direct impact from COVID-19: highest affected (such as restaurants and hotels), moderately affected (such as retail or healthcare), and other industries.

While the U.S. doesn't issue timely GDP statistics on each industry, we can use the employment figures to gauge industry trends in economic activity. Based on the data through May, we project that total U.S. employment will be down 12.5% in the second quarter overall. We think the highest-affected industries will see a 37% hit. Within each industry, we think the fall in GDP will surpass the fall in employment, owing to labor hoarding (companies retaining more workers than needed to carry out operations). In particular, the Paycheck Protection Program strongly encourages companies to hold on to excess workers. Despite this, we expect the aggregate fall in GDP to be less than the fall in employment, as the industries being hit hardest have a much higher share of employment than GDP. The highest-affected industries (for example restaurants, which have a low level of output per worker) account for 15% of U.S. payroll employment though just 6% of U.S. GDP. Altogether, we expect a 10.6% drop in second-quarter GDP (36% on an "annualized" basis, which is most widely quoted in the media).

We expect a sharp GDP rebound in the second half of 2020, with 5.9% growth in the third quarter and 3.2% growth in the fourth quarter (nonannualized). We don't think the need for social distancing will disappear in the second half of 2020, as COVID-19 will still be a lingering threat until a vaccine is broadly available, which we project will occur in the first half of 2021. Still, even while social distancing weighs on highly affected industries, we think the rest of the economy can cope with the ongoing pandemic.

The problem with both the U.S. economy in general and the labor market in particular is not a lack of government stimulus — it's the coronavirus. People are either afraid to work or state governments, to fight the virus, are locking down the businesses where they would work.

As a result, more than 10.7 million people remain out of work and the unemployment rate sits at a relatively high 6.7 percent (although down from 14.7 percent in April). The lockdowns have been particularly hard on the small businesses that employ many of these people. For example, 110,000 restaurants have closed permanently and 500,000 others are in serious trouble, according to a recent National Restaurant Association survey.

Full coverage of the coronavirus pandemic

But that doesn't mean the economy's underlying fundamentals are in crisis. The economy doesn't need massive government spending or programs to revive growth and create jobs. It needs an effective vaccine that finally puts this virus in the rearview mirror.

Economic recovery after COVID-19: the impact on labor and financial markets

The patterns of COVID-19 infection are differing widely across countries and markets. This in turn affects economic outcomes. In this blog we reflect on these differing outcomes and what they might mean for the pace of global economic recovery. Governments around the world have taken different policy stances and strategies for handling the coronavirus pandemic, depending on their circumstances. In this blog, I do not comment on the political response - but make clear that the containment of the virus should be the upmost priority.

What have we seen so far?

There has been considerable debate as to what the shape of economic recovery might look like. Optimistic scenarios point to a rapid "V" shaped recovery, while more pessimistic viewpoints suggest a "U" or even an "L" shaped recovery. While such scenarios are useful in characterizing some of the key issues facing all economies affected by COVID-19, they are also simplistic – recovery patterns are trending differently across key markets (financial, non-financial and labor).

Variable trends across different markets will not combine in an even manner due to inherent differences in each market, their relative health pre-COVID-19 and the design and prioritization of government policy initiatives designed to help offset the health and economic crises.

The most realistic recovery scenario is shaped like a "kinked V" – an initial sharp decline in market activity, followed by a relatively swift bounce back towards pre-COVID-19 levels (once lockdown measures are eased). However, this bounce back won't occur in full. Given the scale of the initial decline most markets will experience long term scarring, meaning that after the initial bounce back there will be an elongated period before markets return fully to pre-COVID-19 levels.

After examining a wide range of data across multiple market segments, differences between the presence and timing of the kinked-V can be seen most starkly in financial and labor markets. These are discussed in turn, but the essence is that in some financial markets the kinked-V has already manifested itself, meaning that they have largely returned to where they were before the pandemic. Labor markets, however, lag significantly behind with evidence from previous recessions illustrating that it may take as long as a decade for normality to return – if at all.

In the more optimistic outcome - the "V-shape": workers' expectations regarding a rapid return to work are fulfilled and only a small proportion become long term unemployed. In the pessimistic outcome - the "L-shape": a high proportion of workers who are temporarily furloughed are not recalled to their pre-COVID-19 job roles. This means they must re-enter the labour market, spend time on job search and possibly even re-skill. This outcome would lead to a much longer recovery timeline.

Perhaps the most likely outcome is somewhere between the two. Initial, tentative signs of a bounce back can be seen in the US unemployment data. In Chart 2, 2020 data for May and June show a rapid reduction in unemployment levels of 13.3% and 11.1% respectively – a +3% shift even with lockdowns still in place in many US states. This is well ahead of the Hall and Kudlyak estimates.

However, a combination of a broad range of factors might limit this bounce back and point to a kinked-V recovery more in line with Hall and Kudlyak. Factors driving the slower paced recovery could be: employer cost-cutting measures leading to job destruction, fundamental changes in working process needed to prevent the spread of COVID-19, the structurally weak state of labor markets and household earnings growth going into the COVID-19 crises, the time-lags and costs associated with re-skilling and a sharp adjustment in how workers and employers use their workforces (e.g. more working from home, streamlined operational processes etc.).

The contrasts between the pace of adjustments in financial and labor markets are stark, but perhaps also unsurprising. While stock market indices seem to be recovering quite quickly, the labor market effects could take a up to a decade to be fully realized. The question then becomes: what scale of feedback loop is there between these two markets? A weaker labor market will put further downward pressure on product and service demand which could in turn lead to hysteresis, weaker equity markets, lower business earnings and reduced overall economic growth.

While the risk of a full downward employment-demand-price spiral (a hysteresis type effect) is relatively low, it could manifest itself in lower incomes for poorer households and widening inequality which was one of the key outcomes of the 2008 crisis. A second-round feedback loop into financial markets should also not be ruled out as this picture becomes clearer. Policy makers should seek to avoid this outcome and invest now in bolstering labor market opportunities for those whose jobs and earnings potential are negatively affected by the COVID-19 crisis.

While the labor market is certainly not as vibrant as it was in 2019, both the number of people unemployed and the unemployment rate are at about the same level they were in early 2014, a full five years into President Barack Obama's administration and 4½ years after the recession ended. I doubt that then-Vice President Biden thought that was a jobs crisis.

Even during the pandemic, the economy has generated a historic increase of 12.3 million jobs since April. The third quarter's 33.1 percent gross domestic product growth rate was an unexpected historic high, and the Atlanta Fed's GDPNow model is forecasting a very strong growth rate, 11.2 percent, for the fourth quarter.

There are already jobs available that could be filled if people felt safe working. At the end of October (the most recent month for which data is available), the economy had 6.7 million job openings. That's more than in any month during the entire Obama administration, and over a million more than when Obama and Biden left office. The real crisis is a lack of workers, not a lack of jobs.

According to the National Federation of Independent Businesses' monthly survey for the end of November, finding qualified employees was the No. 1 problem businesses faced. Nearly half of these businesses hired or tried to hire employees, and nearly 90 percent of them reported few or no qualified applicants.

For now, though, with the approval and widespread distribution of coronavirus vaccines, the U.S. economy would be free to soar as Americans return to work, with no need for even more government stimulus spending. But that will happen only if the next president resists the urge to use the pandemic to "fundamentally transform" America by implementing programs that swell the government rather than the economy.

India's economy shows signs of recovery as Covid-19 cases decline

Business Activity Activity in India's dominant services sector expanded for a third straight month in December, although at a slower pace. The Markit India Services Purchasing Managers' Index came in at 52.3 in December from 53.7 a month earlier.

Consumer Activity Passenger vehicle sales, a key indicator of demand, rose nearly 14% in December from a year ago, with two-wheeler sales witnessing robust growth. The Reserve Bank of India said in its latest monthly bulletin that the employment s...

Industrial Activity Industrial production shrank 1.9% in November from a year earlier. Production of capital goods declined 7.1%, although infrastructure and construction goods showed a slight expansion of 0.7% from a year ago.

Hence, it seems that India's economy ought may have rapid recover more than US's economy after COVID 19 disease disappears because, during nowadays COVID 19 disease is happening, India's economy is significant more stable to compare US's economy nowadays. So, I believe that when COVID 19 disease disappears, India's economy can recover more rapid and easier to compare US's economy.

CHAPTER SIX

www.ingramcontent.com/pod-product-compliance
Ingram Content Group UK Ltd.
Pitfield, Milton Keynes, MK11 3LW, UK
UKHW041639190726
13854UKWH00006B/2588

9 798886 848007